'I would be lost without the books.'

Carly Logan

'My Dad downloaded social media at 65 to start using the recipes.'

Natalie Baird

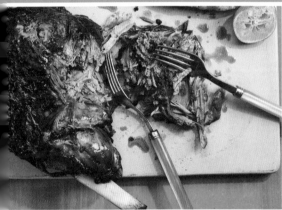

'Simple, speedy meals the kids ACTUALLY eat.'

Charlie Gibson

'Everyday cooking is no longer a chore.'

Chris Law

'Inspired me to cook and keep at it.'

Ellie Clarke

BORED
OF
LUNCH

Healthy Slow Cooker

EVEN
EASIER

BORED OF LUNCH

OF

LUNCH

Healthy Slow Cooker

EVEN EASIER

NATHAN ANTHONY

EBURY PRESS

CONTENTS

Introduction

Wow, how are we at our third *Bored of Lunch* book already? The last couple of years have been a whirlwind and I want to thank every one of you who has supported me on social media and who has bought my books. It's all down to you that I've been able to continue doing what I love, so thank you.

For some of you, this may be your first *Bored of Lunch* book, so if you are new here, hello! I set up Bored of Lunch three years ago as a place to share recipes while I was working from home and increasingly stuck for ways to change up how I was eating every day. As someone with a busy nine-to-five, I wanted to create healthy, delicious food that didn't take ages to prep. Fast forward a few years and my online community has grown to 3 million followers and I've published two number one bestselling books – not bad for a lockdown food blog started in my kitchen.

It's no secret that I love a kitchen appliance, and when it comes to fuss-free, minimal-prep dishes, there's nothing better than a slow cooker. Stick all your ingredients in, switch it on, go about your busy day and come back to a delicious home-cooked meal. Using less energy than a conventional hob or oven, it's also an incredibly cost-effective and efficient way of cooking. Win-win.

I know that what a lot of you loved about my first book was how easy the recipes were. So, for this slow cooker book, I wanted to give you recipes that are even easier! As many 'throw-and-go' recipes as possible (zero prep, just put everything in and go), tips and tricks to make things even quicker (pre-chopped veg, anyone?) and no hard-to-find or specialist ingredients.

Once again, I've included calorie counts for every recipe and each one comes in at under 500 calories per portion (more about this on page 11). Calories are simply something I find useful to track, and I know a lot of you found it helpful to have this included in my first two books. If calories just aren't important to you, then please feel free to up the quantities of oil, butter, cheese etc. These are recipes to make your own!

Chapters include ideas for Meal Prep, Batch and Freeze, Midweek Meals and, of course, my beloved Fakeaways, as well as recipes for Brunch, Soups and Lighter Meals, Comfort Food and Feeding a Crowd. I hope this book will transform the way you and your family cook and eat. I can't wait to see you all recreating these recipes at home.

Love,
Nathan

SLOW COOKER TIPS & TROUBLESHOOTING HACKS

1 Make your life easier and fill the slow cooker the night before if you have no time the next day. The meat or sauce will marinate overnight, giving an even better flavour. If your slow cooker doesn't fit in the fridge, simply add the ingredients to a freezer bag and empty it into your slow cooker in the morning.

2 When cooking meat, ensure you cut it into strips or chunks all the same size so you get a very even cook.

3 For recipes that usually require a lot of spice, go slightly easier than usual with the heat – these recipes cook on a low heat for a long time, enhancing the flavour, so the spice levels can go up because of the long cooking duration.

4 This is such an important one – always add less liquid or stock than you think you need; it is so much easier to add more if required, but it's difficult to take away extra or to thicken larger quantities of liquid.

5 Cooking times may vary depending on what size or brand of slow cooker you own. Use the cooking times I've given you as a guide but keep an eye on it – if something looks dry, add more liquid than I've told you to.

6 Cornflour is something every slow cooker user should have in the pantry. If you need to thicken your sauce, cornflour is your saviour.

7 You can also use a clean tea towel if your dish is looking a little watery. Just drape it over the top of your slow cooker, replace the lid and the tea towel will absorb steam and moisture to help dry things out. It's also useful if you're cooking something like chicken and want to crisp it up a little.

8 If you're adding veg such as peppers or broccoli and you prefer a slightly crunchier texture, add them to your slow cooker for the final 15 minutes or so. If you don't have time and want to add them in with everything else, that's fine, the texture will just be much softer.

9 Cream-based products are less likely to split if the temperature of the sauce is cooler, which is why they're usually added towards the end of cooking.

10 Save yourself time and cut corners everywhere you can, food should be delicious not painfully time-consuming. I do this by using shortcuts such as pre-chopped frozen veg or jars of lazy garlic. You don't have to buy these, you can get ahead by batch peeling and chopping veg like potatoes and then freezing them in bags to defrost and use when you need. For chopping onions, I have a small, inexpensive plastic gadget that chops an onion in 10 seconds.

11 When hosting dinner guests, some slow cookers give you the option to keep warm, so you can get your dish ready and then switch to that setting until you want to serve. If you don't have a 'keep warm' setting, switch to low for 45 minutes max – any longer and sauces or meat can start to dry out.

HOW TO USE THIS BOOK

The recipes in this book have been designed to make cooking as fuss-free and easy as possible and, in particular, to reduce the amount of planning. To help with this, I've included some handy symbols so you can see at a glance if a recipe is suitable for freezing, if it's veggie or if it's going to need less than 5 minutes of hands-on prep time (depending on how fast you chop!).

 freezable

 vegetarian

 5 minutes prep time

When it comes to freezing and defrosting, the important thing is to ensure your food has cooled to room temperature before putting it in the freezer, and then to make sure you reheat everything thoroughly until it's piping hot throughout. Do not refreeze food that has already been defrosted once.

For those of you who are new here and don't have my first slow cooker book, at the back I have included a list of my pantry essentials – the ingredients I find it helpful to have in my cupboard. You can find this on page 184.

A NOTE ON CALORIES – I don't come from a fitness background and I'm not a nutritionist, but I do track my calories to suit my nutritional needs and goals. There are lots of apps that will recommend your ideal calorie intake based on your height and weight (as a general guide, the NHS recommends 2,000 calories per day for women and 2,500 for men). Each recipe in this book comes in at under 500 calories per portion, so that this book can be useful for you if you're trying to tailor your diet to a specific target, while still leaving you plenty of room for snacks throughout the day. However, if calorie counting isn't something that's important to you, feel free to up the portion sizes or make swaps that suit you. For example, I use low-calorie oil spray in most of my recipes that use oil, but if you prefer to use olive oil, please do. If I've only used 100g of chorizo in a recipe but you are a chorizo-lover, please up the amount! If I've said a recipe serves four but you want to split it between two, go for it. I want you to be able to play around with these recipes so that they suit your tastes and lifestyle.

Finally, if a serving suggestion has been included in the ingredients list (e.g. rice, pasta or noodles), then this will be included in the final calorie count. If I've listed something as optional (including optional serving suggestions), this isn't included in the total.

FAKEAWAYS

CHICKEN PAD THAI

PER SERVING
407
CALORIES

I absolutely love a Pad Thai and this version makes it so easy to replicate outside of a wok. I have tried many, many times to cook the noodles in the slow cooker by adding some extra chicken stock to make this a true one-pot dish, but the best result is achieved when you add the cooked noodles at the end.

SERVES **4**

300g chicken breasts, sliced
1 shallot, finely chopped
1 red pepper, chopped or
    sliced
handful of bean sprouts
handful of sugar snap peas
200g dried egg noodles
1 sliced red chilli, handful
    (about 30g) of chopped
    roasted peanuts, lime
    wedges and fresh
    coriander, to garnish

Sauce
2 tbsp rice vinegar
1 tbsp brown sugar
1 tsp fish sauce
juice of 1 lime
2 tbsp oyster sauce
2 tbsp dark soy sauce
100ml chicken stock
3 garlic cloves, grated

1   Add the chicken, shallot and all the sauce ingredients to the slow cooker. Cook on high for 3 hours or low for 5 hours.

2   For the last 20–30 minutes, add the pepper, bean sprouts and sugar snap peas.

3   Cook the noodles separately, then stir through the chicken and garnish with the chilli, peanuts, lime wedges and coriander.

BLACK PEPPER BEEF

PER SERVING
421
CALORIES

The best part of writing a cookbook is getting to test and eat all these recipes, I won't lie. Some of them take several tries, but this beef in a rich sauce with chunky peppers and onions was practically perfect the first time I ever made it. It's reliable, packs a flavour punch and will make you think you are genuinely eating a takeaway.

SERVES **4**

500g beef steak (rump or any cut will do), sliced or cut into chunks
2 tbsp dark soy sauce
100ml chicken stock, plus extra if needed
2 tbsp light soy sauce
1 tsp sesame oil
1 tbsp hoisin sauce
2 onions, cut into chunky pieces

1 tsp pepper
1 tbsp cornflour
1 red pepper, cut into chunky pieces
1 green pepper, cut into chunky pieces
salt, to taste
125g cooked basmati rice per person, to serve

1   Add all the ingredients, except the chopped peppers and rice, to the slow cooker. Cook on high for 3 hours or low for 5–6 hours. Longer is fine if you are out all day.

2   For the last 30–40 minutes or so, add in your peppers. If you like a bit of a crunch, go for 30 minutes.

3   Serve with rice.

SERVING NOTE

This is great served with some steamed Tenderstem broccoli.

TANDOORI MASALA CAULIFLOWER

PER SERVING
381
CALORIES

Cauliflower can be a bit of a love or hate vegetable but I think even the naysayers will love this. The cauliflower cooks slowly, soaking up all these fragrant spices, resulting in a gorgeously warm dish that will convert the non-cauli lovers among us. This is a great veggie dish, packed with goodness; your gut will thank you for this one.

SERVES **4**

2 tbsp tandoori masala powder
1 tbsp ground turmeric
4 garlic cloves, crushed or sliced
1 large cauliflower, cut into florets
1 onion, finely chopped
1–2 x 400g tins of chopped tomatoes

400ml tin of reduced-fat coconut milk
½ tsp ground cinnamon
1 tbsp mango chutney
1 tsp curry powder
1 tsp honey
salt and pepper, to taste
125g cooked basmati rice per person, to serve

1   Add all the ingredients except the rice to the slow cooker. If you don't want it creamy, omit the coconut milk and add 2 tins of chopped tomatoes instead. Cook on high for 3 hours or low for 5 hours.

2   Serve with rice.

TIP

If you buy pre-chopped onion and garlic, it will make this even quicker.

BUTTERNUT SQUASH & SWEET POTATO MADRAS

This is another delicious veggie recipe to have up your sleeve if you're cutting back on your meat intake. My version does use beef stock; however, you can switch it out for veggie stock to make it a completely vegetarian dish, the colour will be slightly lighter but it'll taste just as good. While I use squash and sweet potato here, you can use any other chunky veg that will hold its shape, or add chickpeas or lentils to bulk it out.

SERVES **4**

350g frozen butternut squash, in chunks

300g sweet potato, peeled and chopped

1 onion, finely chopped

4 garlic cloves, sliced or crushed

1 cinnamon stick

400g tin of chopped tomatoes

1 tbsp tomato purée

250ml rich beef stock (or vegetable stock if you're vegetarian)

1 tsp curry powder

1 tsp chilli powder

1 tsp garam masala

1 tsp ground cumin

juice of 2 limes

handful of fresh coriander, chopped, plus extra to garnish

pickled red onion and chopped red chilli, to garnish

150g steamed rice per person, to serve

1 Add all the ingredients, except the garnishes and rice, to the slow cooker. Cook on high for 4 hours or low for 6–7 hours. You can cook the curry for longer but it means your veggies will be a lot softer and won't hold their shape as well.

2 Serve with steamed rice and garnish with fresh coriander, pickled red onion and chilli.

CHICKEN CURRY & NOODLES

Curry once a week is a must in my house, and I always really love serving it with noodles. This is a real quick and dirty one but I honestly love it. The curry sauce is similar to a recipe in my first book but in this dish the noodles are cooked directly in the sauce, making it a true one-pot recipe.

SERVES **4**

3 chicken breasts, sliced

400ml tin of reduced-fat coconut milk

2 tbsp curry powder

1 tbsp ground turmeric

1 tsp ginger purée

1 tsp sliced red chilli

1 tsp ground coriander

½ tsp Chinese 5 spice

2 tbsp tomato purée

5 garlic cloves, crushed or 1 tsp lazy garlic

1 onion, chopped

200g dried egg noodles

350ml chicken stock (optional)

1 tbsp cornflour mixed with 1 tbsp water (optional)

salt and pepper, to taste

1   Add all the ingredients, except the noodles, stock and cornflour, to the slow cooker. Cook on high for 4 hours or low for 6 hours.

2   Stir and add the noodles and stock. (Alternatively, you can skip this step and cook the noodles in a separate pan of boiling water on the hob according to the packet instructions.) If the sauce hasn't thickened, add the cornflour. Close the lid and cook on high for 15 minutes, stirring after 10 minutes. You may need to add a tiny bit more water as the noodles will absorb the curry sauce and stock quickly.

TIP
—

This is best served fresh; I've never made it for meal prep.

BEEF CHOW MEIN

PER SERVING
430
CALORIES

One thing I'll never get bored of is making every fakeaway possible in my slow cooker, and this is one of my favourites. Chow mein is traditionally made with stir-fried vegetables, so obviously this is slightly different as it's made in the slow cooker. Everything cooks down for hours, resulting in a deep, intense flavour and there's minimal oil and no sugar used, making it much healthier than a traditional takeaway.

SERVES **4**

400g beef, such as rump or any cheap thin steak, sliced
1 onion, chopped
3 garlic cloves, crushed or sliced
small thumb-sized piece of fresh ginger, grated or chopped (I use frozen)
2 tsp sesame oil
2 tbsp oyster sauce
1 tsp hoisin sauce
4 tbsp dark soy sauce

1 tbsp rice wine
100ml chicken or beef stock
1 tbsp cornflour
3 spring onions, sliced
200g sugar snap peas
1 carrot, cut into matchsticks
200g dried egg or rice noodles, cooked according to packet instructions
pepper, to taste
1 tbsp sesame seeds, to garnish

1   Add all the ingredients, except the carrot and noodles, to the slow cooker. Cook on high for 3–4 hours or low for 6 hours.

2   Add the carrot for the last 30 minutes of cooking, then stir in your cooked noodles. Divide between bowls, top each with a sprinkling of sesame seeds and enjoy.

LAMB & POTATO CURRY

This is truly a dump-and-go recipe. You don't even need to peel the potatoes or boil the kettle for the stock. It couldn't be easier, and the resulting curry is stunning. It packs in the flavour, and the fresh mint at the end gives it a real lift. It's gorgeously filling too, so will stretch far portion-wise.

SERVES **4**

300g lamb, cut into chunks

6 potatoes, chopped into chunks

4 garlic cloves, crushed or sliced

400g tin of chopped tomatoes

1 tbsp tomato purée

400ml tin of reduced-fat coconut milk

1 tsp ground cumin

1 tsp garam masala

1 tbsp curry powder

1 tsp ground ginger

1 tsp ground turmeric

1 tbsp mango chutney

2 bay leaves

1 lamb or chicken stock pot

1 onion, chopped

1 tbsp cornflour mixed with 1 tbsp water (optional, if you want a thick sauce)

salt, to taste

shredded fresh mint leaves, to garnish

125g cooked basmati rice per person, to serve (optional)

1   Add all the ingredients, except the mint and rice, to the slow cooker. Cook on high for 4 hours or low for 8 hours. If your sauce is looking a little thin at the end of the cooking time, stir in the cornflour mixture.

2   Top with some fresh mint and serve with rice.

TIP

This is a very versatile recipe, swap out the lamb for chicken breast or beef rump if you fancy.

STICKY BUFFALO CHICKEN WINGS

PER SERVING
345
CALORIES

This is the laziest way to get yourself flavoursome chicken wings without paying a fortune. I flex between making wings in my air fryer and my slow cooker, but on a busy working-from-home day, this method is a regular: simply chuck it all in and come back to deliciously sticky wings, perfect for dunking in a blue cheese dip.

SERVES **6**

1kg chicken wings, skin on
1 tsp paprika
½ tsp baking powder
½ tsp dried coriander
1 garlic clove, grated
4 tbsp buffalo sauce
1 tbsp honey

1 tbsp sweet chilli sauce
salt and pepper, to taste
chopped spring onions,
    sliced red chilli and juice
    of 1 lime, to garnish
blue cheese dip and celery
    sticks, to serve (optional)

1   Pat the chicken wings dry with some kitchen paper.

2   In a bowl, coat the wings in the paprika, baking powder, coriander, grated garlic and some salt and pepper. Then coat in the buffalo sauce, honey and sweet chilli sauce.

3   Add the wings to the slow cooker and cook on high for 3 hours or low for 5 hours. (I find placing a tea towel on top of the slow cooker under the lid helps to get the wings crispy.)

4   Garnish with spring onions, chilli and lime juice. Serve with blue cheese dip and celery sticks, if you like.

TIP
—

If you want these extra crispy, at the end, put your oven-safe slow-cooker pot under a hot grill (without the lid) for 5–6 minutes before glazing with some of the extra sauce from the bottom of the slow cooker.

SPICY THAI RED VEGGIE CURRY

PER SERVING
490
CALORIES

Who doesn't love Thai Red Curry? It's one of the all-time greats and so easy to make at home. Most people think of a Thai red curry being made with chicken but this is a delicious veggie version. You won't even be able to tell there's meat missing, the veg just simmers away in this incredible curry sauce.

SERVES **4**

3 large sweet potatoes, peeled and chopped
400ml tin of reduced-fat coconut milk
400ml passata
2 carrots, cut into chunks
1 onion, chopped
2 tbsp light or dark soy sauce
2 tbsp honey
1 tbsp sriracha
1 tsp chilli flakes, plus extra if you like it spicy
4 tbsp Thai red curry paste or 4 paste pots

1 tbsp tomato purée
3 garlic cloves, grated or chopped
thumb-sized piece of fresh ginger, grated
juice of 1 lime
handful of sugar snap peas
salt and pepper, to taste
fresh coriander and grated lime zest, to garnish
125g cooked rice per person and (optional) flatbreads, to serve

1   Add all the ingredients, except the sugar snap peas, garnishes and rice, to the slow cooker. Cook on high for 2–3 hours or low for 5–6 hours.

2   For the last hour of cooking, add the sugar snap peas so they still retain a slight crunch.

3   Top with fresh coriander and lime zest for some punch. Serve with rice and flatbreads to mop up that sauce, if you like.

STICKY SWEET & SPICY CHICKEN

This is a slow cooker version of one of my Chinese takeaway favourites – General Tso's Chicken. Traditionally a deep-fried dish, you don't get that classic crunch of the fried chicken here but the taste is next level. I use chicken thighs here to make it a bit more cost-effective, and the rest of the ingredients might already be things you have in your cupboards. I love serving this with rice but it's also delicious with ramen noodles.

SERVES **4**

400g boneless and skinless chicken thighs, cut into small pieces
1 tbsp cornflour
6 tbsp dark soy sauce
100ml chicken stock
1 tbsp honey
1 red chilli, chopped
1 tsp hoisin sauce
1 tsp rice vinegar

1 tbsp tomato purée
1 tsp sesame oil
1 tbsp garlic purée
1½ tsp ginger purée
small grinding of black pepper, to taste
1 tsp sesame seeds and chopped spring onions, to garnish
150g cooked ramen noodles per person, to serve

1   Coat the chicken thighs in the cornflour.

2   Add to the slow cooker with all the remaining ingredients, except the garnishes and the noodles. Cook on high for 4 hours or low for 6 hours.

3   Serve with the ramen noodles, garnish with the sesame seeds and spring onions and enjoy.

BEEF ADOBO & BROCCOLI

PER SERVING
452
CALORIES

Adobo is the national dish of the Philippines and I absolutely love it. Essentially, it's a way of marinating meat in a mixture of vinegar, soy sauce and spices before cooking slowly to create a rich, flavourful stew. I love adding my vegetables to the slow cooker towards the end of the cook time to save on having to prep sides separately. In this case I've gone for broccoli, but feel free to switch this up for whatever you prefer.

SERVES **4**

600g beef, such as rump or any cut you can get, sliced
150ml beef stock
1 heaped tbsp cornflour
1 head of broccoli, cut into florets, or 200g Tenderstem broccoli
125g cooked rice per person, to serve

Sauce
2 tbsp brown sugar
juice of ½ lime
4 tbsp dark soy sauce
2 tbsp light soy sauce
3 tbsp rice vinegar
4 garlic cloves, sliced
1 red chilli, sliced
handful of black peppercorns
2 tbsp honey
2–3 bay leaves

1   Add the beef to a freezer bag with all the sauce ingredients and marinate in the fridge for at least 6 hours, or overnight if possible.

2   Add the marinated beef, beef stock and cornflour to the slow cooker. Cook on high for 2–3 hours or low for 5–6 hours.

3   If using thicker broccoli florets, cut up and add to the slow cooker for the last hour of cooking. If using Tenderstem broccoli, add for the last 40 minutes. Serve with cooked rice.

BUTTER CHICKEN

PER SERVING
439
CALORIES

Butter Chicken is one of my absolute favourite curries but restaurant versions do tend to be very calorific. This is a great alternative to make at home and, if you're not worried about calories, feel free to use full-fat butter or increase the amount that's added. I tend to use half-fat butter to reduce calories where possible, but just go for whatever makes sense for your diet. I also use yogurt instead of cream to finish the curry as a lower-fat alternative but, as always, just go with your preference.

SERVES **4**

4 chicken breasts, cut into chunks
4 garlic cloves, grated
50g half-fat butter
1 tbsp ground turmeric
1 tbsp garam masala
1 heaped tbsp curry paste of your choice
1 tsp ground cumin

2 x 400g tins of chopped tomatoes
1 onion, finely sliced
4 tbsp yogurt (or double cream if you're feeling more luxurious)
fresh coriander, to garnish
8 chapatis, to serve

1   Add all the ingredients, except the yogurt and serving suggestions, to the slow cooker. Cook on high for 4 hours or low for 7–8 hours.

2   Stir in the yogurt (or cream).

3   Top with fresh coriander and serve with two chapatis per person.

STICKY WHISKEY BBQ RIBS

PER SERVING
352
CALORIES

It's no surprise that whiskey and barbecue sauce is a phenomenal combination, perfect for burgers or ribs or to spice up some roasted veggies. I have listed the ingredients here to make your own barbecue sauce from scratch, but you could skip this and just use a ready-made jar.

SERVES **6**

1–1.5kg pork ribs
salt and pepper, to taste
chopped spring onions and
    fresh coriander, to garnish

Sauce
25ml whiskey (I use Jack
    Daniel's)
8 tbsp reduced-sugar
    tomato ketchup

3 tbsp Worcestershire sauce
2 tbsp dark soy sauce
1 tsp Tabasco sauce
80ml apple cider vinegar or
    rice wine vinegar
100ml pineapple juice
1 tbsp tomato purée
3 tbsp brown sugar
2 tbsp molasses or honey

1   Add the ribs to the slow cooker and season with salt and pepper, then throw in all the sauce ingredients. (Or you can mix 100ml of shop-bought barbecue sauce with 25ml of whiskey.) Cook on high for 4 hours or low for 7 hours.

2   For an extra crispy result, pop the ovenproof slow-cooker pot (without the lid) under a hot grill for 10 minutes. If your slow-cooker pot isn't oven-safe, transfer the ribs to a baking tray and place under the grill instead.

3   Garnish with spring onions and coriander to serve.

SERVING NOTE

I love these with some coleslaw and creamed corn on the side.

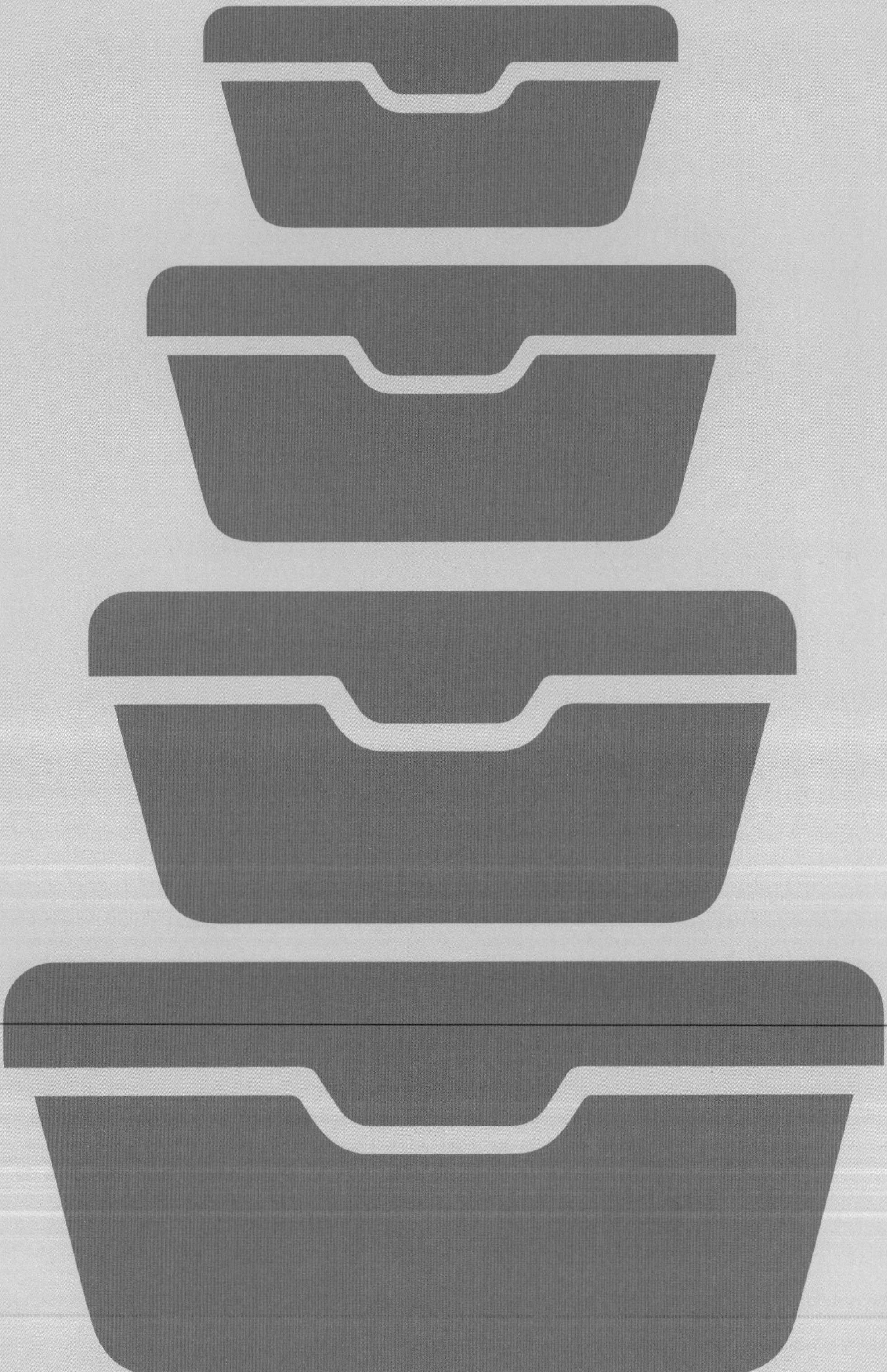

MEAL PREP,

BATCH

&

FREEZE

TERIYAKI BEEF BOWLS

PER SERVING
442
CALORIES

When I say this is one of my go-to meal preps, you can bet it appears a few days every month. It's perfect if you want to plan ahead; simply throw and go, then box up and freeze. A cheaper and healthier alternative when you find yourself craving a sticky and sweet takeaway.

SERVES **4**

500g lean beef steak, cut into strips
4 tbsp dark soy sauce or tamari
2 tbsp light soy sauce
3 tbsp honey
1 tsp sesame oil
1 tbsp mirin
1 tsp chilli flakes
3 garlic cloves, grated
1 tsp ground ginger

1 heaped tbsp cornflour, (optional, if you want a thicker sauce)
chopped spring onions, 1 tsp mixed sesame seeds and a sliced red chilli, to garnish
125g sticky boiled or steamed rice per person, to serve
grated carrot, edamame beans and a sliced lime (optional), to serve

1   Throw all the ingredients into the slow cooker, except the garnishes and serving accompaniments. Cook on high for 3–4 hours or low for 5–6 hours.

2   Serve with rice. I love adding some grated carrot and edamame beans and a lime slice per bowl. Garnish with spring onions, mixed sesame seeds and chilli slices.

SERVING NOTE

Noodles also work really well here instead of rice.

SAAG ALOO

PER SERVING
282
CALORIES

This is another dish that is perfect for batch cooking and to use as you like throughout the week; either as a side with a protein of your choice or served with chapati or dal as a veggie main. You can also transform this into a flavourful potato curry by adding a tin of coconut milk and another of chopped tomatoes in with the rest of the ingredients.

SERVES **4**

1kg Maris Piper potatoes, peeled and cut into small chunks

1 tsp mustard powder (I use Coleman's)

1 tbsp olive oil

1 tbsp tomato purée

150ml vegetable stock

½ thumb-sized piece of fresh ginger, grated

1 tsp ground coriander

1 tsp curry powder

1 tsp ground cumin

1 tsp ground turmeric

4 garlic cloves, chopped or grated

1 onion, chopped

2–3 large handfuls of spinach (or more to taste)

fresh coriander, to garnish

1 red chilli, chopped, to garnish

1 Add all the ingredients, except the spinach, coriander and chilli, to the slow cooker and cook on high for 2 hours 20 minutes or low for 5 hours. Stir in the spinach for the last 10 minutes or so.

2 Garnish with some fresh coriander and red chilli.

CAJUN-STYLE DIRTY RICE with spiced pork

PER SERVING
374
CALORIES

I love dirty rice, and this is gorgeous with well-seasoned strips of pork. It's quite a cheap dish and such a simple one to rustle up, which makes it even better. You can change up the veg and use green beans or broccoli, but I like it with peppers. Simple but loaded with flavour.

SERVES **4**

500g pork chops or pork
   tenderloin, thinly sliced,
   fat removed
1 onion, chopped
1 tbsp hot sauce
1 tsp dried coriander
1 tsp ground cumin
1 tsp chilli flakes
1 tsp celery salt
1 tbsp Cajun seasoning

1 tbsp garlic purée
1 tbsp Worcestershire sauce
1 tbsp dark soy sauce
850ml chicken stock
150g easy-cook rice, rinsed
1 yellow pepper, sliced
1 green pepper, sliced
salt and pepper, to taste
chopped spring onions and
   fresh coriander, to garnish

1   Toss the pork strips and onion in the hot sauce, spices, garlic purée, Worcestershire sauce and soy sauce.

2   Add all the remaining ingredients, except the rice and peppers, to the slow cooker with 100ml of the stock. We don't want to boil the meat, just let it simmer gently.

3   Cook on high for 3 hours or low for 6 hours, then add the rice and remaining 750ml of stock and cook for 45 minutes on high or 1 hour on low. Add the peppers, stir and cook for a further 15 minutes (this is the same time if cooking on high or low).

4   Garnish with spring onions and coriander and enjoy.

LAMB KOFTA CURRY

Like a lot of people, I love lamb koftas, which are delicious on their own or with flatbreads. However, here I'm sharing a recipe I created one Sunday when I was feeling slightly delicate after the night before. I was craving koftas but I also wanted a curry, and this recipe is the result. This is so quick to prep, and the meatballs don't need any breadcrumbs or egg, making it even easier.

SERVES **4**

Meatballs
500g lean lamb mince
1 tbsp desiccated coconut
1 tsp chilli powder
1 tsp onion granules
1 tbsp garlic purée or lazy
   garlic

Curry sauce
1 tbsp curry powder
1 tbsp your favourite curry
   paste

1 tsp ground cumin
1 tsp ground coriander
1 tsp garam masala
500g passata
1 tbsp tomato purée

To serve
125g cooked basmati rice
   per person
fresh coriander
lime wedges
green chilli, sliced
garlic naan (optional)

1   Mix together all the ingredients for your meatballs. Roll into meatballs. Heat a frying pan over a medium heat on the hob and seal the meatballs for around 1 minute. You could also use an air fryer, just put them in at 200°C for 8 minutes.

2   Add the meatballs and the curry sauce ingredients to the slow cooker and cook on high for 4 hours or low for 7 hours.

3   Serve with rice, fresh coriander, lime wedges and green chilli slices, and the garlic naan, if you choose.

RED PEPPER BRUSCHETTA PASTA

PER SERVING 493 CALORIES

This is another recipe I came up with when trying to decide between two favourite dishes. In this case, bruschetta and pasta. The result is this soft pasta with lots of flavour, crunchy croutons and a drizzle of balsamic: stunning. I do enjoy making my own sourdough croutons in the air fryer or the oven, but shop-bought croutons work very well if you don't have the time.

SERVES **3**

2 x 300g jars of roasted red peppers, chopped
15 cherry tomatoes, quartered
700g passata
1 tsp dried oregano
4 garlic cloves, grated
generous handful of fresh basil

250g fresh lasagne sheets, cut into thick strands
salt and pepper, to taste
4 tsp balsamic vinegar, croutons and 50g grated vegetarian Parmesan cheese, to serve

1   Add the peppers, tomatoes, passata, oregano, grated garlic, salt and pepper and most of the basil to the slow cooker. Cook on high for 2 hours or low for 4 hours.

2   Add the lasagne strands and cook for a further 20–25 minutes (if cooking on low, you may need slightly longer).

3   Plate up and top the pasta with the balsamic vinegar, croutons, Parmesan and remaining fresh basil.

TIP

To make your own sourdough croutons, cube a couple of slices of bread, toss them in olive oil and put in the air fryer at 200°C for 6 minutes, or on a baking tray in a 200°C oven for 10–12 minutes.

CREAMY VEGGIE BAKE

PER SERVING
377
CALORIES

It might sound very bizarre to use tinned soup in a recipe like this but, trust me, the end result is so good. This is similar to a recipe I posted online that used chicken soup and leftover Christmas turkey, so feel free to play around with whatever you choose here. You can decrease the amount of veg and add in chicken breasts if you prefer a meat version but, whatever you do, it makes either a brilliant side dish or main event.

SERVES **4**

2 carrots, chopped

2 leeks, chopped

2 sweet potatoes, chopped (peeling optional)

1 onion, chopped

1 head of broccoli, broken into florets

2 parsnips, peeled and chopped

2 x 400g tins of cream of mushroom soup (or creamy chicken soup if you're not veggie)

1 tbsp Dijon mustard

150ml vegetable stock

juice of 1 lemon

1 tbsp cornflour, mixed with 1 tbsp water, to thicken (only if required)

80g breadcrumbs

20g vegetarian Parmesan cheese, grated

salt and pepper, to taste

1   Add all the ingredients, except the cornflour, breadcrumbs and cheese, to the slow cooker and cook on high for 2½ hours or low for 5 hours.

2   If your sauce is looking a little thin, add the cornflour mixture. Top with the breadcrumbs and Parmesan and pop the ovenproof slow-cooker pot (without the lid) under a hot grill for 8–10 minutes until golden and crisp. Serve and enjoy.

CHILLI CON CARNE MACARONI MELT

I am honestly obsessed with this dish. If chilli con carne, pasta bake and macaroni cheese all went in one pot, then this would be the result. There's no need to brown the mince, just chuck everything in and go, perfect if you are out all day or want to get ahead during a busy time. You can make this veggie by replacing the beef with Quorn mince, or using lentils and extra veg instead.

SERVES **5**

400g lean beef mince
700g passata
1 tbsp tomato purée
3 garlic cloves, grated or chopped
handful of fresh coriander, chopped, plus extra to garnish
1 red chilli, sliced
1 onion, chopped
1 packet of chilli con carne spice mix (or you can make your own)

700ml chicken stock
400g tin of kidney beans, drained and rinsed
1 red pepper, chopped
250g dried macaroni
120g Cheddar cheese (get reduced-fat if you can), grated
salt and pepper, to taste

TIP

To make your own chilli con carne spice mix, use a teaspoon each of ground cumin, paprika, ground cinnamon and chilli powder.

1   Add the beef mince, passata, tomato purée, garlic, half the coriander, the chilli, onion, chilli con carne spice mix and salt and pepper to the slow cooker. Cook on high for 4 hours or low for 7–8 hours.

2   Add the stock, kidney beans, red pepper and macaroni and cook on high for a further 45 minutes. If cooking on low, you'll need to leave it for closer to 1 hour to cook the pasta.

3   Stir through half the Cheddar into the dish, top with the remainder, then garnish with the remaining coriander. Absolutely stunning.

TOMATO, CHICKPEA & PESTO ORZO

PER SERVING
493
CALORIES

I could eat orzo every day – I love it. This dish can be served hot on a chilly night but is also really nice cold as a pasta salad on a summer's day. It feels like a classic spring or summer dish. There is virtually no prep required here: all you need to do is halve the cherry tomatoes and you're done.

SERVES **4**

200g cherry tomatoes, halved
400g tin of chickpeas, drained
400g tin of chopped tomatoes
4 garlic cloves, grated
1 tsp onion granules
1 tbsp basil pesto

1 tsp dried oregano
350g dried orzo
900ml vegetable stock, plus extra if needed
90g light soft cream cheese (I use Philadelphia)
salt and pepper, to taste
chopped fresh basil leaves, to garnish

1   Add three-quarters of the halved cherry tomatoes to the slow cooker, saving some for the last 15 minutes of cooking.

2   Add all the remaining ingredients, except the soft cheese and basil, to the slow cooker and cook on high for 70 minutes or low for 2 hours.

3   Stir in the remaining cherry tomatoes and soft cheese for the last 15 minutes of cooking.

4   Garnish with fresh basil and serve.

TIP
▬

Adding some sundried tomatoes to this dish takes it to another level.

BUFFALO CHICKEN PASTA BAKE

PER SERVING
499
CALORIES

I love spicy buffalo chicken and it goes so well in this all-in-one pasta dish. This is another 'throw-and-go' recipe with hardly any prep – simply chuck everything in the slow cooker and off you go. You don't even need to boil the pasta separately, you can just add it in towards the end of the cooking time. So simple and so tasty. I like to serve this with a side of guacamole.

SERVES **4**

400g chicken breasts, sliced
1 tsp paprika
100ml hot sauce (I use Frank's RedHot Buffalo Wings Sauce)
400g tin of chopped tomatoes
1 onion, finely chopped
3 garlic cloves, grated

325g dried penne
650ml chicken stock
3 heaped tbsp light soft cream cheese
60g grated mozzarella and Cheddar mix
salt and pepper, to taste
sliced jalapeños, soured cream and chopped chives, to garnish

1 Place the chicken, paprika, hot sauce, chopped tomatoes, onion, garlic and salt and pepper into the slow cooker and cook on high for 2½ hours or low for 4 hours.

2 Add your pasta and stock and cook on high for 50 minutes or low for 1 hour, stirring after 30 minutes. Then stir in the soft cheese.

3 Top with the grated cheese and pop the ovenproof slow-cooker pot (without the lid) under a hot grill for 7 minutes. If your slow cooker isn't oven-safe, then top with the grated cheese and just let the cheese melt in the slow cooker with the lid on.

4 Garnish with sliced jalapeños, soured cream and the chopped chives.

SPICY CHIPOTLE PULLED BEEF BOWLS

PER SERVING
485
CALORIES

I can't tell you how many times I've made this, but it is a lot. I debated putting this recipe in the Feeding a Crowd chapter as it's so good when you've got people round, but it's also a perfect meal prep and freeze dish. I tend to batch-cook it, freeze and then defrost portions to take into the office, which I jazz up with microwaveable rice packs and coriander.

SERVES **8**

1.2kg beef brisket
1 tbsp Cajun seasoning
low-calorie oil spray
3 tbsp chipotle paste
500ml beef stock
juice of 2 limes, plus grated zest and juice of 2 limes (optional, for the rice)
1 tsp paprika
1 tsp curry powder (I use mild)

3 tbsp garlic purée or 3 garlic cloves, grated
1 bay leaf
salt and pepper, to taste
125g cooked basmati rice per person, chopped avocado, chopped tomato, chopped red onion and sliced (bottled) jalapeños, to serve

1   Coat the beef in the Cajun seasoning. Heat a frying pan over a medium heat on the hob, spray with low-calorie oil spray and seal the beef for 2 minutes.

2   Add to the slow cooker with all the remaining ingredients, except the serving accompaniments, and cook on high for 6–7 hours or low for 9–10 hours. Discard the bay leaf.

TIP

—

I use my onion chopper for the tomatoes at the end to save time.

3   When cooking the rice, squeeze the juice of 2 limes into the water, then grate in the zest, if you like.

4   Shred the beef with two forks, then pair the pulled beef with 125g cooked rice per person and serve with your toppings of choice.

BEEF STIFADO & ORZO

PER SERVING
492
CALORIES

This rich beef dish is such a perfect dinner when the colder weather arrives. I'm not sure this is the most traditional version of this dish but it is my take on it. The pasta cooks in the sauce so there's no need to boil anything separately. I use orzo because I'm low-key obsessed with it and I think it works so well here, but you can use penne or tagliatelle if you like.

SERVES 4

400g beef rump, cut into chunks or thin strips
2 tbsp tomato purée
1 onion, chopped
1 beef stock pot
300ml boiling water
400g tin of chopped tomatoes
3 carrots, chopped into batons
1 red wine stock pot or splash of red wine
1 tsp mixed spice
½ tsp ground cinnamon

3 bay leaves
1 tsp dried oregano
1 tsp dried basil
1 tsp dried parsley
4 garlic cloves, chopped or crushed
330g dried orzo
700ml beef stock
salt and pepper, to taste
grated Parmesan or other hard cheese, to serve (optional)

1   Add all the ingredients, except the orzo and stock, to the slow cooker. Cook on high for 3 hours or low for 6–8 hours.

2   Add the orzo and stock and cook on high for 45–50 minutes or low for 1 hour until the pasta is cooked and has absorbed the stock. Different shapes of pasta may require more stock, so add more if required.

3   Serve topped with grated cheese, if you like.

BANG BANG CHICKEN NOODLES

Bang bang chicken gets its name because you hammer the chicken to tenderise it before cooking. I love the flavour and first came across it in a sandwich. Since then I have had every possible combo: with rice, noodles, pasta, you name it. I've gone with noodles here but go for whatever you prefer.

SERVES **4**

4 chicken breasts
4 tbsp reduced-sugar sweet chilli sauce
2 tbsp sriracha
1 tbsp smooth peanut butter
2 tbsp dark soy sauce
400ml tin of reduced-fat coconut milk
4 garlic cloves, grated
1 tsp paprika
1 red chilli, finely chopped

1 tsp onion granules
100ml chicken stock
2 red peppers, sliced lengthways
300g cooked egg or rice noodles
salt and pepper, to taste
chopped spring onions, sliced red chilli and fresh coriander, to garnish

TIP
—

Noodles don't freeze that well, so I'd suggest freezing the chicken, then defrosting, reheating and stirring through the noodles just before eating.

1   Add the chicken to a clear plastic bag and give it a few bangs with a rolling pin to flatten, then slice it into strips.

2   Add to the slow cooker with all the remaining ingredients, except the peppers and noodles, and cook on high for 3 hours or low for 5 hours. Add the peppers for the last 20 minutes of cooking.

3   Stir in the cooked noodles, garnish and serve straight away or leave to cool, then put in the fridge to enjoy later.

BRUNCH,

SOUPS

& LIGHTER MEALS

BERRY & COCONUT CRUMBLE

PER SERVING
388
CALORIES

Like many people, I have days when my sweet tooth reaches whole new levels and hardly anything will satisfy it. On those days, I try to make slightly leaner sweet treats to hit that sugary craving, and stop me reaching for the pick 'n' mix. This sweet and moreish crumble served with fat-free frozen yogurt really satisfies.

SERVES **4**

3 tbsp half-fat butter
350g raspberries
300g blueberries
200ml water
50g white granulated sugar
50g granulated sweetener

1–2 tbsp strawberry jam
75g granola
75g flaked almonds or other
   nut of your choice
1 tbsp desiccated coconut

1   Melt the butter in a heatproof bowl in the microwave.

2   Add the melted butter, fruit, water, sugar, sweetener and jam to the slow cooker and mix. Top with the granola and flaked almonds and half the desiccated coconut. Cook on high for 3½ hours or low for 5 hours.

3   Take the lid off and sprinkle with the remaining desiccated coconut, then serve.

CARROT CAKE OVERNIGHT OATS

PER SERVING
400
CALORIES

Overnight oats are a great way to get ahead. Usually served cold out of the fridge, this warm version made in the slow cooker is next level. It's easy to see why this combo has become so popular. A sneaky way to get veggies in at breakfast while at the same time tasting of carrot cake, what's not to love?

SERVES **4**

500ml skimmed milk
150g porridge oats
1 tsp vanilla extract
1 tbsp ground cinnamon
1 tsp ground nutmeg
handful of dried fruit (around 50g), chopped

200g Greek yogurt
2 large carrots, grated
25g chopped walnuts, zest of 1 orange and 4 tbsp honey, to serve

1   Mix all the ingredients, except the walnuts, orange and honey, in your slow cooker. Cook on low for 8 hours. If you're an early riser, throw it all in and cook on high for 3 hours.

2   Serve with the chopped walnuts, orange zest and a drizzle of honey.

TIP
—

If it looks a little dry at any point, add a splash more milk. If cooking overnight, add a few extra splashes at the start so it doesn't dry out.

RICE PUDDING

PER SERVING
280
CALORIES

Rice pudding is one of those dishes that instantly transports me back to being at school. Call me Oliver Twist but I *always* asked for more. My mum had daily cravings for rice pudding when she was pregnant with me, which is probably why I enjoy it so much. Whatever the reason, I love this slow-cooker version. All the nostalgia with none of the faff.

SERVES **6**

170g pudding rice
75g caster sugar
4 tbsp raisins or chopped
   dried fruit of your choice
850ml skimmed milk
1 tbsp vanilla extract

1 tbsp half-fat butter
70ml double cream
6 tsp ground cinnamon, to
   dust the bowls and 6 tbsp
   strawberry jam or a berry
   compote, to serve

1   Add all the ingredients, except the cream, cinnamon and jam, to the slow cooker. Cook on high for 3 hours or low for 4–5 hours, adding the cream for the last 30 minutes of cooking.

2   Serve, then top each bowl with a teaspoon of ground cinnamon and a tablespoon of jam or compote.

SPICED BAKED BEANS
with turkey bacon bits

I've made this a few times and it is so versatile; you can have it for breakfast, brunch or even as a side at dinner. If you're working from home, add a poached egg and some toast for dipping. Turkey bacon is great if you're trying to keep calories down, but it goes without saying that you can substitute it for regular bacon, chorizo or even add some sausages.

SERVES **4**

200g turkey bacon, cut into chunks
2 x 400g tins of cannellini beans, drained
400g tin of kidney beans, drained
600g passata
4 tbsp tomato purée

5 tbsp tomato ketchup
1 tbsp brown sugar
1 tsp chilli flakes
1 tsp garlic granules
salt and pepper, to taste
chopped fresh herbs of your choice, to garnish
slice of sourdough toast each, to serve

1 In a frying pan over a medium heat on the hob, cook the turkey bacon for 2 minutes. (You can skip this step if you're in a rush.)

2 Add to the slow cooker with all the remaining ingredients, except the herbs and toast. Cook on high for 2–3 hours or low overnight (for 7–8 hours maximum).

3 Serve on a piece of toasted sourdough and garnish with fresh herbs.

STICKY APPLE CINNAMON SWIRL PUDDING

PER SERVING
475
CALORIES

Using shop-bought dough rolls was one of those viral trends that I came across and thought wouldn't be nice. I'm happy to say I was wrong! I've played with the recipe to create something sticky and even sweeter and I think you'll love it. This does serve six but three people could easily demolish it.

SERVES **6**

½ tbsp half-fat butter

2 shop-bought cinnamon swirl dough rolls (available from the supermarket fridge section)

2 apples, cored and chopped (I use Granny Smith)

1 tbsp brown sugar

1 tsp ground cinnamon

50ml double cream

270ml skimmed milk

3 egg yolks, plus 1 egg, beaten

1 tbsp icing sugar, for dusting

1   Rub the butter along the base and bottom rim of the slow cooker. Cut each dough roll into 6 circles, then quarter each circle.

2   Mix the apples with the brown sugar and cinnamon.

3   Add half the apple mixture to the slow cooker, then half of the dough. Then add the rest of the apples, and top with the remaining dough. Mix together the cream, milk and egg yolks. Pour over the dough in the slow cooker. Brush the top with the beaten egg.

4   Cover with a tea towel, then the lid, and cook on high for 3 hours. Dust with the icing sugar and enjoy. Heaven.

TIP

I think this works much better cooked at the high setting. If you need to, you could try it on low for 5 hours.

CRISPY GRANOLA

PER SERVING
253
CALORIES

This gorgeous granola makes for such a great yogurt and fruit topper and will have you coming back time and time again. This recipe makes loads, so store it in an airtight jar and you've got breakfast sorted for the week. I also like to snack on handfuls of this when I'm working from home and need a quick energy hit.

SERVES **8**

1½ tbsp half-fat butter
225g porridge oats
2 egg whites, beaten
75g dried fruit of your choice
75g nuts of your choice, chopped

2 tsp ground cinnamon
6 tbsp honey
greek yogurt and fresh fruit, to serve

1   Melt the butter in a heatproof bowl in the microwave for 1 minute.

2   Add to the slow cooker with all the remaining ingredients, except the yogurt and fresh fruit, and cook on high for 2 hours. Stir and cook on high for another hour. Because you're aiming to dry out the ingredients, this recipe is most suited to cooking on the high setting.

3   Transfer to a lined baking tray and leave to cool. Serve with yogurt and fruit.

TIP
—

Store any leftover granola in an airtight container to enjoy for quick breakfasts all week.

CREAMY MUSHROOM SOUP

I adore a mushroom soup, plus it's so easy and cheap to make. I like to serve mine with a drizzle of truffle oil and crunchy garlic bread for dipping, but you could top it with croutons and a swirl of cream instead. Heaven any day of the year.

SERVES **6**

1 tbsp half-fat butter
550g mushrooms, chopped
1 onion, chopped
1 small-medium potato, peeled and chopped
1.3 litres vegetable stock
4 garlic cloves, chopped or crushed
1 tsp celery salt
few sprigs of fresh thyme, leaves picked

handful of fresh parsley, roughly chopped, plus extra to garnish
50ml double cream
3 heaped tbsp light soft cream cheese
salt and pepper, to taste
1 tbsp truffle oil and cream per serving, to garnish
garlic bread or croutons, to serve (optional)

1   If you have time, heat a frying pan over a medium-high heat on the hob and melt the butter. Add the mushrooms and soften for 2 minutes. Add to the slow cooker, reserving 50g of the mushrooms for the garnish, then add all the remaining ingredients, except the cream and soft cheese.

2   Cook on high for 3 hours or low for 4–5 hours. Meanwhile, if you chose not to soften the mushrooms before adding to the slow cooker, do so for the reserved mushrooms as in step 1.

3   After 3 hours on high, add the cream and soft cheese and blitz with a handheld blender.

4   Serve in bowls. Top with the softened mushroom and some parsley, swirl in the truffle oil and cream. Some garlic bread on the side or croutons on top makes this special.

SERVING NOTE

This is a great one to batch-cook and freeze in single portions.

BRUNCH, SOUPS & LIGHTER MEALS

SMOKY MINESTRONE SOUP

PER SERVING
337
CALORIES

Minestrone is such a popular soup and it's not hard to see why. Even better, it's a great one to put your own twist on, depending on what you've got left over in the house – switch up the veg, leave out the beans, change up the pasta shape, whatever you want. I think the chorizo here really gives it a punch and takes the flavour up a notch, but you could use lardons or leave them out and swap the chicken for vegetable stock for a veggie version.

SERVES **7**

150g chorizo, chopped
700g passata
2 handfuls of cherry tomatoes, halved
1.1 litres chicken stock
3 tbsp tomato purée
3 carrots, chopped into small chunks
2 celery sticks, chopped
½ courgette, chopped
3 Maris Piper potatoes, peeled and chopped
1 onion, chopped

1 tsp paprika
2 garlic cloves, grated
150g dried spaghetti, snapped into smaller pieces
400g tin of butter beans (or other beans of your choice), drained
handful of kale, chopped
salt and pepper, to taste
buttered crusty bread, to serve (optional)

1   If you have time, heat a frying pan over a high heat on the hob and cook the chorizo for 1 minute. You can skip this step if you want to speed up the process. Add the chorizo to the slow cooker with all the remaining ingredients, except the spaghetti, beans and kale. Cook on high for 4 hours or low for 7–8 hours.

2   For the last 40 minutes, add the spaghetti, beans and kale.

3   Serve with buttered crusty bread, if you like, and enjoy.

COURGETTE & PARMESAN SOUP

Courgette soup is definitely underrated, but genuinely this is one of the nicest soups I've had in a while. I think most people think courgettes will taste bland but, combined with garlic and herbs and finished with Parmesan, this is really tasty. I urge you to make it, it'll convert even the courgette naysayers.

SERVES **6**

8 courgettes, chopped
5 garlic cloves, crushed
1 tbsp olive oil, plus extra (optional) to serve
1 onion, chopped
1 sprig of fresh oregano
1 sprig of fresh rosemary
1 bay leaf
2–3 potatoes, chopped

1.2 litres stock of your choice (I use chicken)
1 tbsp half-fat crème fraîche
salt and pepper, to taste
40g grated vegetarian Parmesan cheese, and air-fried/baked croutons, to serve

1 If you want the best flavour, mix together the courgettes, garlic, oil and salt and pepper. Roast in an air fryer at 190°C for 20–25 minutes, or in the oven on a lined baking tray at 180°C for 40 minutes. If you want to be super savvy, you can skip this step to save on energy and time, then just add the ingredients directly to the slow cooker and cook for an extra 30 minutes.

2 Add the cooked veg and all the remaining ingredients, except the crème fraîche, Parmesan and croutons to the slow cooker, and cook on high for 3 hours or low for 4–5 hours.

3 Remove the rosemary stalk and bay leaf, blitz with a handheld blender. Stir in the crème fraîche and blitz again.

4 Serve and top with the Parmesan and croutons and more oil, if you like, or just whatever you fancy.

TIP

If you're feeling indulgent, melt a bit of butter into the soup at the end of cooking for a richer, more velvety texture.

IRISH FARMHOUSE CHICKEN & VEG SOUP

PER SERVING 214 CALORIES

Here's an Irish staple soup that is so hassle-free. No need to blitz anything, you just chop your veg, chuck everything in the slow cooker and come back to a beautiful broth with lots of veg, chicken and lentils. This is really filling too, so it's perfect when you want something light to warm your tummy.

SERVES **6**

700g shop-bought chopped mixed veg (around 3 leeks, 3 carrots and 1–2 celery sticks – adjust based on your preference)
300g cooked chicken, shredded
70g dried pearl barley

70g dried red lentils
handful of fresh parsley, chopped
1.4 litres chicken stock (or fill the slow cooker to the top)
salt and pepper, to taste
crusty bread, to serve (optional)

1   Chop the vegetables if needed, cutting the carrots into small chunks.

2   Add all the ingredients, except the bread, to the slow cooker. If I can, I'll add the chicken for the last hour or two but, if not, it's fine to add it at the start. It will just fall apart and become stringy. Cook on high for 3 hours or low for 5 hours.

3   Serve with crusty bread, if you like.

MEXICAN-INSPIRED TURKEY & TORTILLA SOUP

PER SERVING
313
CALORIES

This soup recipe is a holiday in a bowl and perfect for using up leftover turkey, chicken and tortilla wraps. I love this if I'm feeling a bit hungover on Sunday and want to eat something satisfying but don't want the expense and calories of a takeaway. I make this with leftovers, but it's so good, I've definitely cooked myself some turkey purely to make this soup before. It does have a real kick, so if you don't like spice, just reduce or leave out the chilli flakes.

SERVES **6**

1 jalapeño, sliced
1 tsp chipotle paste
1 onion, chopped
½ tsp chilli flakes
1 heaped tsp paprika
2 x 400g tins of chopped tomatoes
650ml chicken or turkey stock
300g tin of sweetcorn, drained
400g tin of black beans, drained

300g cooked turkey or chicken, shredded with two forks
1 square of dark chocolate (optional)
3 tortilla wraps, cut into triangles and cooked at 200°C in an air fryer for 4 minutes or in the oven for 8–10 minutes
fresh coriander, sliced red chilli, lime wedges and 1 tsp soured cream per bowl, to garnish

TIP
—
If you don't have any leftover turkey, simply add a couple of raw turkey breasts to the pot, along with everything at the beginning, then shred before serving.

1   Add all the ingredients, except the turkey, chocolate and tortilla triangles, to the slow cooker. Cook on high for 2 hours or low for 4 hours.

2   About 10 minutes before the cooking time is up, add the shredded turkey and dark chocolate, if using. Then 3 minutes before the end, stir in most of your air-fried tortilla triangles. You can also just crumble them directly on top of the soup bowls.

3   Divide the soup into bowls, garnish and enjoy.

SPICY TOMATO, TORTELLINI & CHILLI SOUP

PER SERVING
184
CALORIES

Tomato soup with pasta, this is real comfort food. You can roast the tomatoes before they go in the slow cooker which will give you a greater depth of flavour but, if you don't have time, you can just throw it all in together and leave it to do its thing. As with all these soup recipes, you can make this on the hob but your slow cooker will save on energy and require less of your attention.

SERVES **6**

12 tomatoes, quartered
2 tbsp tomato purée
2 x 400g tins of chopped
   tomatoes
1 red chilli, sliced
5 garlic cloves, crushed or
   sliced
1 onion, chopped

1 celery stick, chopped
2 carrots, chopped
handful of fresh basil, plus
   extra leaves to garnish
1 tsp dried oregano
1 litre vegetable stock
250g shop-bought fresh
   tortellini of your choice
salt and pepper, to taste

1   If you have time, preheat the oven to 180°C. Add the tomatoes to a baking tray and roast for 25 minutes.

2   Add to the slow cooker with all the remaining ingredients, except the tortellini. Cook on high for 3 hours or low for 5 hours.

3   Blitz with a handheld blender, then stir in your tortellini and cook on high for 10–15 minutes. Serve in bowls, garnished with extra basil leaves.

TIP

The better the quality of ripe tomatoes you can find, the tastier this soup will be.

FRAGRANT CHICKEN NOODLE SOUP

I love a chicken noodle soup and I make this one regularly. You have the option of using leftover chicken or poaching the chicken in the hot broth while you go about your day, the smell is so inviting. The bean sprouts and noodles bulk this soup out, making it very filling while also stretching the portions further.

SERVES **6–7**

1.5 litres chicken stock

zest and juice of 1 lime

3 bay leaves

3 tbsp dark or light soy sauce

handful of fresh basil or 1 tbsp Thai basil, if you can find it

3 garlic cloves, grated

½ thumb-sized piece of fresh ginger, grated

3 chicken breasts (left whole) or 300g leftover cooked chicken

1 tbsp honey

300g dried rice noodles

300g tin of sweetcorn or peas, drained

75g bean sprouts

handful of pak choi, leaves left whole

3 large spring onions, chopped, plus extra to garnish

salt and pepper, to taste

fresh coriander, lime wedges and chilli oil, to garnish

1   Add all the ingredients, except the noodles, sweetcorn, bean sprouts, pak choi and spring onions, to the slow cooker. (If using cooked chicken, only add it when the noodles go in.) Cook on high for 3 hours or low for 5 hours.

2   For the last 15 minutes, add the noodles, sweetcorn, bean sprouts, pak choi and spring onions.

3   Use two forks to pull the chicken apart, then divide the soup between bowls and garnish with extra spring onions, fresh coriander, lime wedges and chilli oil.

PEA & MINT SOUP

PER SERVING
234
CALORIES

Truth be told, even though I try to do some batch cooking and meal prepping on a Sunday, some weeks I just don't get round to it. This soup is what I make when I've just run out of time but don't want to fall back on pre-made supermarket soup. This recipe is absolutely zero prep, everything goes into the slow cooker together and the result is this gorgeously fresh soup that can be enjoyed all year round. Light but filling and full of greens, your body will thank you.

SERVES **6**

handful of chopped fresh mint, plus extra to garnish
650g frozen peas
1 onion or shallot, chopped
1–1.2 litres vegetable stock, plus extra if needed
200ml skimmed milk (optional)

1 potato, chopped
juice of 1 lime
3 garlic cloves, crushed
salt and pepper, to taste
6 tbsp shaved vegetarian Parmesan cheese, pea shoots and pumpkin seeds or chopped nuts, to garnish

1   Add all the ingredients, except the garnishes, to the slow cooker. If you don't want to add the milk, use 1.2 litres of stock instead. Cook on high for 3 hours or low for 5–6 hours.

2   Blitz with a handheld blender, then serve in bowls and garnish with the Parmesan, pea shoots, pumpkin seeds and extra mint.

MIDWEEK MEALS

VEGETARIAN ENCHILADAS

PER SERVING
419
CALORIES

When making enchiladas, adding tortillas or corn snacks directly into the slow cooker is a great hack to turn it into a one-pot dish. However, I think toasting them beforehand helps them maintain a bit of their crunch. You can fold and toast them in your toaster or add them to your air fryer, whichever is easiest.

SERVES **5**

1 large carrot, finely chopped

400g tin of kidney beans, drained

400g tin of cannellini beans, drained

1 onion, finely chopped

250g sweet potatoes, peeled and chopped (I buy mine frozen and pre-peeled)

200g courgettes, chopped

1 tsp dried oregano

1 tsp dried sage

1 tsp paprika

1 tsp chilli powder

1 tbsp curry powder

5 garlic cloves, chopped or grated (I use lazy or frozen garlic)

1 tbsp balsamic vinegar

1 tbsp honey

700g passata

400g tin of chopped tomatoes

1 tbsp tomato purée

5 small corn tortillas

70g reduced-fat Cheddar cheese, grated

salt and pepper, to taste

1   Add all the ingredients, except the tortillas and cheese, to the slow cooker. Cook on high for 4 hours or low for 8 hours.

2   About 10 minutes before the filling is ready, fold your tortillas and toast them in a toaster or cut them into quarters and place in an air fryer. Stir them through the slow cooker, top with the cheese and cook for a further 10 minutes. Serve and enjoy.

THAI-STYLE TURKEY LETTUCE CUPS

PER SERVING
443
CALORIES

During the month of January, this recipe becomes one of my go-to meals. It is obviously carb-conscious, so is a helpful dish to have up your sleeve to beat the post-Christmas bloat, but you can make these all year round and vary them up with soft shell tacos. To make them extra filling, add a supermarket packet of pre-cooked rice to the lettuce cups to bulk them out.

SERVES **4,**
2 PER PERSON

500g turkey mince
1 tbsp Thai basil paste, or
  1 tbsp dried basil and 1 tsp
  chilli flakes
1 lemongrass stalk, sliced
1 tsp fish sauce
3 tbsp sriracha
3 garlic cloves, grated
1 tbsp hoisin sauce

2 tbsp honey
1 tbsp dark soy sauce
zest and juice of 1 lime
150ml chicken stock
8 lettuce leaves
chopped red chilli, spring
  onions and fresh coriander,
  to garnish
125g cooked basmati rice per
  person, to serve

1   Add all the ingredients, except the lettuce, garnishes and rice, to the slow cooker, ensuring the turkey mince is well broken up with your spoon, or even cut through it with scissors to help break it up (my tip to you). Cook on high for 3½ hours or low for 6 hours.

2   Serve in the lettuce cups, with rice as extra filling, and your chosen garnishes.

TIP
—

The turkey filling will freeze, but the lettuce cups won't, they'll need to be fresh.

SPICED LAMB FLATBREADS

I love a flatbread and I love lamb, it's a combination that just transports me briefly to somewhere with a warmer climate than Belfast, Northern Ireland. This version here, served with a spicy yogurt, is one of my favourites. The mint really balances the heat from the harissa, so it works really well as a combo. This is perfect for four people with some leftovers, or it will feed six people comfortably.

SERVES **6**

800g lean lamb leg, diced
  (or a full leg on the bone)
2 tbsp harissa paste
1 tbsp garlic purée
1 tsp garam masala
1 tsp curry powder
1 tsp ginger purée
1 tsp ground cumin
juice of 1 lemon
150ml lamb stock

flatbreads, julienned
  cucumber and lime
  wedges, to serve

Harissa & mint yogurt
1 tsp harissa paste
5 tbsp fat-free Greek yogurt
chopped fresh mint leaves
juice of ½ lime

TIP
—

If you're using a leg on the bone, you might need a 6.5l slow cooker but, if you're going with diced lamb, your 3.5l pot will be fine.

1   Coat the lamb in the harissa, garlic purée and spices, then add to the slow cooker with the lemon juice and stock. Cook on high for 4 hours or low for 8 hours.

2   I like a bit of a char on the outside of my lamb, so pop the ovenproof slow cooker (without the lid) under a hot grill for 10 minutes to help it crisp up.

3   Mix together all the ingredients for the harissa and mint yogurt. Serve the lamb (pulled into pieces with two forks if you cooked it on the bone) with flatbreads, julienned cucumber, lime wedges and the harissa and mint yogurt. Beautiful.

CAJUN CHICKEN & PENNE ALFREDO

PER SERVING
497
CALORIES

It's no secret that I'm a bit obsessed with Cajun chicken, and it popped up a few times in my air fryer book, but here I've paired it with creamy, cheesy pasta. This is incredibly easy to make and I guarantee the whole household will love it. It really does jazz up those midweek meals, which can be a bit repetitive if you don't have time to try something new.

SERVES **4**

400g chicken breasts, flattened with a rolling pin
2 tbsp Cajun seasoning
generous amount of low-calorie oil spray or 1 tbsp olive oil (I use light olive oil)
500ml chicken stock
2 good handfuls of fresh parsley, chopped
1 tbsp lazy garlic or 4 garlic cloves, crushed
1 shallot, chopped
1 tsp ground nutmeg

25g half-fat butter
1 heaped tbsp cornflour
1 tsp dried oregano
½ tsp paprika
250g dried penne
400ml skimmed milk
2 tbsp light soft cream cheese
30g reduced-fat mozzarella, torn into chunks
1 tbsp grated Parmesan cheese
salt and pepper, to taste

1   Coat the chicken in 1 tablespoon of the Cajun seasoning. Heat a frying pan over a medium heat on the hob, spray with low-calorie oil spray or add the tablespoon of oil. Add the chicken and cook for 1 minute on each side.

2   Slice the chicken, and add it to the slow cooker with the stock, half the parsley, the garlic, shallot, nutmeg, butter, cornflour, oregano, paprika and salt and pepper. Cook on high for 2½–3 hours or low for 5 hours.

3   Add the pasta and milk and cook on high for 50–60 minutes or low for 70 minutes; pasta usually cooks

quicker but the milk is cold, so it needs more time to reach temperature.

4   Stir in the soft cheese, mozzarella and Parmesan and sit the sliced chicken breasts on top of the penne. Cook for another 10 minutes.

5   Garnish with the remaining parsley and enjoy.

COTTAGE PIE

PER SERVING
499
CALORIES

Cottage pie is such a classic from my childhood and there's nothing more comforting on a cold winter's night. Rich beef soaked up by cheesy creamy mash, so if that doesn't make your mouth water, then I'm not sure what will. You can make the mash your own way here but, if you're feeling extra lazy, you can use supermarket pre-made mash (we have all used this sneaky hack).

SERVES **4**

600g lean beef mince
400g tin of chopped
   tomatoes
1 onion, chopped
100ml beef stock
50ml red wine, mixed to a
   paste with 1 tbsp cornflour
1 tbsp Worcestershire sauce
4 garlic cloves, grated
1 bay leaf

2 sprigs of fresh rosemary,
   leaves picked and chopped
2 tbsp tomato purée
2 carrots, finely chopped
1 celery stick, finely chopped
700g mashed potato with
   50g grated reduced-fat
   Cheddar cheese
salt and pepper, to taste

1   If you have time and prefer an even more intense flavour, brown the mince in a frying pan over a medium heat on the hob for 2 minutes, breaking it up as you go.

2   Add all the ingredients, except the mash, to the slow cooker. Cook on high for 5 hours or low for 7–8 hours, then remove the bay leaf and rosemary sprigs.

3   Top with your cheesy mash, or just the mash and then top with grated cheese – I like piping my mash on for effect. Pop your ovenproof slow-cooker pot (without the lid) under a hot grill for 7 minutes until golden and crisp. Serve and enjoy.

CHICKEN, BACON & LEEK CASSEROLE

PER SERVING
486
CALORIES

Say hello to your new favourite casserole, perfect for autumn and winter. It's as cheap as chips and takes no effort to make. Chicken, bacon and leek in a creamy white wine sauce, what could be better? You could easily add a pastry lid to this to make a pie instead of serving it with mash (or go for both!).

SERVES **4**

low-calorie oil spray
8 smoked bacon medallions, cut up with scissors
400g chicken thighs (left whole)
3 small leeks, roughly sliced
100ml white wine
300ml chicken stock
2 tbsp cornflour, mixed to a paste with 2 tbsp water
1 tbsp wholegrain mustard
few sprigs of fresh rosemary

handful of fresh oregano, chopped
1 tsp dried parsley
3 garlic cloves, crushed or 1 tbsp garlic purée
1 tbsp crème fraîche or double cream
salt and pepper, to taste
150g mashed potato and 80g green beans per person, to serve

TIP

—

This will stretch to 5 servings because there are two types of protein, then your veg and mash. Or for those who are extra hungry, make 4 large servings.

1   Heat a frying pan over a medium heat on the hob. Add a few sprays of low-calorie oil spray, add the bacon and cook for 2 minutes.

2   Add all the ingredients, except the mash and beans, to the slow cooker. Cook on high for 4 hours or low for 7–8 hours. If you need the sauce thicker, add more cornflour.

3   Shred the chicken thighs. Serve the casserole with mash.

TOMATO & MASCARPONE RISOTTO
with sticky halloumi

PER SERVING
496
CALORIES

If you have read my other books, you will have heard me harp on about how every week I struggle to not eat an entire block of halloumi cheese. So, why not add it instead to a gorgeous risotto with tomatoes and mascarpone? I mean, who doesn't love two types of cheese with their risotto? This is absolute perfection – adding that sweet and sticky halloumi on top of the risotto really elevates this midweek staple.

SERVES **4**

300g risotto rice
400g tin of chopped
 tomatoes
1 litre hot vegetable stock,
 plus extra if needed
200g cherry tomatoes,
 halved
handful of fresh basil leaves,
 plus extra to garnish
½ tsp paprika

3 garlic cloves, chopped or
 grated
35g mascarpone (or light soft
 cream cheese)
200g reduced-fat halloumi,
 sliced
2 tbsp sweet chilli sauce
salt and pepper, to taste
chopped sundried tomatoes,
 to garnish

TIP
—

When freezing rice, ensure it is fully defrosted and thoroughly reheated before eating.

1 Add all the ingredients, except the mascarpone, halloumi and sweet chilli sauce, to the slow cooker. Cook the risotto on high for 2 hours or low for 3–4 hours.

2 About 5 minutes before the risotto is cooked, stir through the mascarpone. Coat the halloumi slices in the sweet chilli sauce and cook in a small frying pan for a few minutes until they become darker and sticky, soaking up that sweet chilli sauce.

3 Add the risotto to serving bowls, then add the halloumi. Top with chopped sundried tomatoes and fresh basil.

CHIPOTLE CHICKEN & PRAWNS

I am a little bit obsessed with the flavour of chipotle – it's one of my go-to pastes when I'm in a hurry and want to add a bit of kick to my dinner. Prawns, chicken and coriander in this creamy spiced sauce is a killer combo and it's so easy, it pretty much makes itself. If you want to skip the chicken and add veg to make it a pescetarian dish, that will work equally well.

SERVES **4**

2 chicken breasts, cut into chunks
1 tbsp half-fat butter
3 tbsp chipotle paste
500g passata
1 tbsp smoked paprika, plus extra to garnish
½ tsp mild chilli powder (if you like extra heat)
1 shallot, finely chopped

4 garlic cloves, crushed
handful of fresh coriander, roughly torn, or 1 tbsp ground coriander, plus extra (fresh) to garnish
150g raw peeled king prawns
100g light soft cream cheese
salt and pepper, to taste
125g cooked basmati rice per person, to serve

1   Add all the ingredients, except the prawns, soft cheese and rice, to the slow cooker.

2   Cook on high for 2 hours or low for 5 hours.

3   Pop in the prawns and cook on high for a further 1 hour or low for 90 minutes, then stir through the soft cheese. Simply serve with rice, garnished with fresh coriander and a small sprinkle of smoked paprika to make it pop for the eager waiting eyes.

PAPPARDELLE ALLA BISTECCA

PER SERVING
440
CALORIES

This recipe is inspired by a restaurant from my hometown and every time I go there, I order this dish. Rich sauce with steak, mushrooms and fresh pasta really is in a league of its own. Gorgeous! The pasta is cooked directly in the sauce which makes things so much easier.

SERVES 4

1 tsp half-fat butter (optional)

2 x 250g lean steaks (extra-thick sirloin is best)

2 tbsp red wine

1 shallot, finely chopped

250g mixed fresh porcini and chestnut mushrooms, sliced

1 tsp dried sage

1 bay leaf

small handful of fresh basil, plus extra to serve

350ml rich beef stock, plus extra if needed

3 garlic cloves, crushed or sliced

300g fresh lasagne sheets, cut into thick pappardelle-style strips

1 heaped tbsp low-fat crème fraîche or light soft cream cheese

1 tbsp cornflour (optional)

salt and pepper, to taste

20g Parmesan cheese shards, to serve

1 If you like, melt the butter in a searing hot pan on the hob and flash-fry the steaks for less than a minute on each side.

2 Add the steaks and the remaining ingredients, except the lasagne sheets, crème fraîche or soft cheese and cornflour, to the slow cooker. Cook on high for 3 hours or low for 5 hours.

3 Remove the steaks and the bay leaf. Add the fresh pasta strips, then cook on high for a further 20 minutes, or low for 30 minutes. Stir in the crème fraîche or soft cheese. Cut the steaks into slices and return to the slow cooker for 3–4 minutes until they absorb some of the sauce. If the sauce is too thin, mix the cornflour with 1 tbsp water and stir it into the sauce.

4 Serve topped with the Parmesan shards and extra basil.

TIP
—

If you can't find porcini mushrooms, you can simply use 250g chestnut mushrooms.

CREAMY TIKKA MASALA COD

Is there anything nicer than flaky cod in a gorgeous curry sauce? I love serving this with plenty of sauce to go round and fluffy naan to soak it up. I find it both a really light but filling dish. Cod is a low-calorie fish and is packed full of goodness; a win-win.

SERVES **4**

TIP
—

This is also great served with rice or cubed potatoes cooked in the air fryer at 200°C for 20 minutes or in the oven for 30–35 minutes.

4 skinless cod fillets
400ml tin of reduced-fat coconut milk
300g passata or 400g tin of chopped tomatoes (I use passata because it's smoother, so there's no need to blitz the sauce)
1 tbsp tikka masala paste (any supermarket version will do)
2 tbsp garlic purée
1 tsp ginger purée
1 tbsp honey
juice of 2 limes

1 tsp onion granules
½ tsp ground cumin
½ tsp mild chilli powder
1 tbsp cornflour mixed with 1 tbsp water, to thicken (if required before serving)
lime wedges, sliced green or red chilli, handful of cashew nuts and handful of fresh coriander, to garnish
80g steamed green beans and 1 mini naan per person, to serve

1   Add all the ingredients, except the cornflour and garnishes, to the slow cooker and cook on high for 2–3 hours or low for 5 hours. Don't stir this recipe as you want the cod fillets to remain whole and absorb that gorgeous tikka masala sauce.

2   Using a spatula, carefully remove the cod fillets from the slow cooker to serving bowls so they don't fall apart. If the sauce is too thin, stir through the cornflour. Pour the sauce over the fish. To each bowl, add a lime wedge, some fresh chilli, cashew nuts and fresh coriander.

3   Serve with naan and green beans.

BURRATA LINGUINE

PER SERVING
499
CALORIES

Just run and make this, don't lose any time reading this introduction, it doesn't need one. It's pasta and burrata, need I say more? Stunning and completely mouth-watering, the sauce bubbles away all day, gaining in flavour before the pasta goes in for a bath and it's all topped with oozy burrata. Perfect with crusty bread for dipping.

SERVES **4**

500g passata
2 tbsp balsamic vinegar
1 tsp chilli flakes
½ tsp paprika
1 bay leaf
1 tsp dried oregano
2 handfuls of sundried
  tomatoes, chopped
1 onion, chopped
4 garlic cloves, crushed
  or 1 tbsp garlic purée
handful of fresh basil,
  chopped, plus extra
  to garnish

300g dried linguine (or
  penne or pasta of your
  choice)
800ml vegetable or chicken
  stock
1 burrata, drained and torn
  into pieces
salt and pepper, to taste
1 tsp olive or chilli oil per
  person and chopped
  pistachios, to garnish

1   Add all the ingredients, except the pasta, stock and burrata, to the slow cooker. Cook on high for 3 hours or low for 6–7 hours.

TIP

Feel free to add two extra burrata, but the calories will naturally go up.

2   Add the pasta and stock and cook on high for a further 50 minutes, checking halfway to ensure you don't need any more stock, and moving the pasta around with a fork.

3   Add the pasta to individual bowls or a large bowl, top with the burrata pieces, drizzle with the olive or chilli oil, garnish with basil leaves and chopped pistachios and ENJOY.

SAUSAGE, FENNEL & BACON RAGÙ

PER SERVING
469
CALORIES

When you hear 'ragù', I think most people instantly think of beef. However, here's a slightly different version made with sausage and bacon. It's so moreish and satisfying and the flavour is next level. If you need to stretch this dish for more than four people, this recipe doubles up really well.

SERVES **4**

200g bacon medallions, sliced (I use scissors)
6 low-fat pork or turkey sausages, skins removed
1 tbsp crushed fennel seeds
2 x 400g tins of chopped tomatoes
1 tbsp tomato purée
1 tbsp Worcestershire sauce
100ml red wine

300ml beef stock
1 tbsp brown sugar
1 tsp dried oregano
1 tbsp dried basil
500g cooked pasta of your choice
fresh thyme sprigs and 20g grated Parmesan cheese, to garnish

1   In a frying pan over a medium heat on the hob, cook the bacon and sausage meat with the crushed fennel for 2 minutes until browned, breaking up the sausage meat as you go.

2   Add to the slow cooker with all the remaining ingredients, except the pasta, and cook on high for 4 hours or low for 8 hours.

3   Toss in the cooked hot pasta, then serve, topped with the thyme and Parmesan.

ROAST CHICKEN & VEG DINNER

This will be the easiest roast chicken dinner you can make and will save you a fortune on your energy bills. Everything cooks in the slow cooker together: the chicken, potatoes, carrots and gravy, so no worrying about timings and making sure everything is ready at the same time.

SERVES **4**

3 large potatoes, cut into chunks

3 carrots, chopped chunky (too small and they will be too soft)

1 medium chicken (around 1kg)

handful of mixed fresh rosemary and thyme

3 garlic cloves, peeled and left whole

150ml chicken stock

low-calorie oil spray

sprinkle of dried Italian seasoning

1 tsp half-fat butter

1 tsp ground nutmeg

2 tbsp gravy granules or powder

salt and pepper, to taste

1   Add your potatoes and carrots to the slow cooker and rest the chicken on top. Add the fresh herbs, garlic and stock. Spray the chicken with low-calorie oil spray and sprinkle with the Italian seasoning and some salt and pepper. Cook on high for 5 hours or low for 7–8 hours.

2   Baste the chicken in the cooking juices, then pop the ovenproof slow-cooker pot (without the lid) under a hot grill for 10 minutes to crisp up the chicken.

3   Remove the chicken from the slow-cooker pot and set aside to rest, then remove your potatoes and carrots, separating them out.

4   Melt the butter and nutmeg in a heatproof bowl in the microwave and toss the carrots in this mixture.

5   Mix the juices at the bottom of the slow cooker with your gravy granules or powder. Carve the chicken and serve with the carrots, potatoes and gravy.

FESTIVE BEEF, RED WINE & CRANBERRY STEW

PER SERVING
492
CALORIES

This dish is such a nice twist on a classic stew using more festive ingredients. You can also add potatoes to it if you prefer but I think it goes so well with creamy, buttery mash. A rich beef stew with some sweetness from the cranberries, it delivers the goods and is a nice change from turkey dishes or leftover turkey sandwiches over the festive period.

SERVES **4**

500g beef (rump steaks work best), cut into small pieces
1 onion, chopped
150g fresh cranberries
500g potatoes, peeled and chopped (optional)
500ml beef stock, plus (optional) an extra 300ml if adding potatoes to the slow cooker
200ml red wine
1 tbsp cranberry sauce

2 sprigs of fresh rosemary
4 carrots, chopped
4 garlic cloves, chopped
1 bay leaf
1 tbsp tomato purée
2 heaped tbsp gravy powder
1 tbsp cornflour mixed with 1 tbsp water (optional)
salt and pepper, to taste
175g creamy mashed potato per person and cooked cabbage wedges, to serve

1   Add all the ingredients to the slow cooker, including 2 heaped tablespoons of gravy powder. Cook on high for 4 hours or low for 8 hours. If you would like to thicken the sauce, add the cornflour towards the end.

2   Discard the bay leaf and rosemary sprigs, then serve with cabbage and creamy mashed potato if you haven't added the potatoes to the slow cooker.

COMFORT FOOD

MUSSELS WITH 'NDUJA
in a creamy sauce

This is one of those dishes that works as well for a light lunch as it does for an impressive dinner for friends. For me, there's nothing more comforting than dunking bread in this creamy sauce, and the combo of garlic, white wine, mussels and 'nduja is hard to beat. 'Nduja is available in most supermarkets but, if you can't find it, chorizo is a great replacement.

SERVES **4**

100g 'nduja or chorizo, crumbled or chopped

1 tbsp half-fat butter

generous handful of chopped fresh parsley, plus extra to garnish

1 shallot, finely chopped

juice of 1 lemon

70ml white wine

1 vegetable stock pot or cube, mixed with 100ml boiling water

4 garlic cloves, grated, or 1 tbsp garlic purée

½ tsp black pepper

1kg fresh mussels in shells, or frozen, defrosted

100ml double cream

salt, to taste

lemon wedges and a slice of sourdough bread, per person, to serve

1   Add all the ingredients, except the mussels and cream, to the slow cooker. You want the broth to cook for a few hours to allow the flavours to develop, ready for those mussels to join. Cook on high for 2–3 hours or low for 4–5 hours.

TIP

If you're using fresh mussels, make sure you discard any that remain closed after cooking them.

2   Add the mussels and cream, close the lid and cook on high for a further 35–45 minutes or low for 1 hour until the mussels have opened. Discard any that haven't opened.

3   Add to your bowls, ensuring you spoon over that creamy garlic broth for dipping.

4   Garnish with parsley and serve with lemon wedges and lots of crusty bread to soak up that sauce.

TURKEY SAUSAGE JAMBALAYA

PER SERVING
459
CALORIES

This gorgeous rice and sausage dish will really fill you up and give you a taste of summer at the same time. Switch up the protein if you want – it works amazingly with prawns, chicken, chorizo or a combination of all three. I absolutely love this and it's a perfect choice for meal prep to help keep you organised, on plan and on budget. There's a fair bit of chopping in the prep, but once you're done it's pretty much throw in and go.

SERVES **4**

low-calorie oil spray

8 turkey sausages (around 300g – chicken, pork or veggie are also fine)

400g tin of chopped tomatoes

1 green pepper, chopped

1 red pepper, chopped

1 celery stick, chopped

1 jalapeño, chopped

handful of cherry tomatoes, halved

4 tbsp tomato purée

1 onion, chopped

2 tbsp Cajun seasoning

1 tsp paprika

1 tsp dried oregano

4 garlic cloves, crushed

½ tsp chilli flakes

2 tbsp hot sauce of your choice (I use Frank's RedHot Buffalo Wings Sauce)

1 tbsp Worcestershire sauce

260g long-grain rice

900ml hot chicken stock, plus extra if needed

chopped spring onions and fresh parsley, to garnish

1   Spray a frying pan set over a high heat on the hob with low-calorie oil spray, then add the sausages and seal for 1-2 minutes.

2   Add to the slow cooker with all the remaining ingredients, except the rice and stock. Cook on high for 3 hours or low for 6 hours.

3   Add the rice and hot stock and cook for a further 1 hour, keeping an eye on it. Depending on the type of the rice that you use, you might need more stock, so give it a stir after 40 minutes.

4   Serve, garnished with spring onions and parsley, and enjoy.

PULLED BEEF, ONION & GRAVY SANDWICHES

PER SERVING
451
CALORIES

This is one of those lazy, can't-be-bothered recipes that you can dump in the slow cooker and leave to do its thing. Perfect if you're out at work all day and want to come home to something comforting. A kilo of brisket will make quite a lot, so go for a lower weight if you want to yield fewer portions. I love having this in sandwiches, but you can serve it with potatoes, pasta or on its own with a salad.

SERVES **7**

1 tsp half-fat butter
800g–1kg beef brisket (in one piece)
4 onions, sliced
low-calorie oil spray (optional)
1 tbsp brown sugar
1 tsp dried thyme or oregano
1–2 bay leaves
1–2 tbsp Worcestershire sauce
100ml white wine

400ml beef stock
2 garlic cloves, crushed (optional)
1 heaped tbsp cornflour
1 heaped tbsp gravy powder, mixed with 1 tbsp water (add more at the end if the sauce needs to be thicker)
salt and pepper, to taste
7 ciabatta rolls with butter, to serve

1   Melt the butter in a frying pan over a high heat on the hob and brown the beef briefly. Remove to a plate (or the slow-cooker pot). Using the same pan, soften the onions. There should be enough butter left over, or you can use some low-calorie oil spray if needed.

2   Add all the ingredients to the slow cooker, except the bread rolls, and cook on high for 7–8 hours or low for 12 hours.

3   Shred the beef with tongs or two forks and serve.

4   Lightly toast the halved ciabatta rolls, spread with butter, then fill with the beef mixture. Serve with extra gravy on the side to dip for pure heaven, if you like.

HUNTER'S CHICKEN
with Parma Ham

PER SERVING
496
CALORIES

Loosely inspired by Hunter's Chicken, this is heaven on a wet day. Chicken wrapped in Parma ham, slow-cooked in a delicious sauce and finished with a cheesy lid. This is another one of those speedy recipes that is perfect for when you are in a mad dash. Just quickly throw this together before heading out of the door.

SERVES **4**

4 chicken breasts
4 slices of Parma ham (use more if you like)
1 onion, chopped
4 garlic cloves, crushed or grated
1 tsp paprika
1 tbsp Italian herb seasoning
500g passata
1 tbsp tomato purée

4 tbsp barbecue sauce (any will do or you could make your own)
80g reduced-fat mozzarella, shredded or grated
1 tbsp grated Parmesan cheese
salt and pepper, to taste
100g air-fried homemade chips and 80g green beans per person, to serve

1   Wrap your chicken breasts in the Parma ham and add on top of the onion in the slow cooker.

2   Add all the remaining ingredients, except the cheeses, chips and beans, and cook on high for 4 hours or low for 7 hours.

3   Add the mozzarella and Parmesan cheese on top for the last 15 minutes of cooking. If you like, pop the ovenproof slow-cooker pot (without the lid) under a hot grill for 7 minutes to brown the cheese. Serve with the chips and green beans.

TIP
—

If you don't have an air fryer, baked oven chips are a great alternative.

COMFORT FOOD

CHORIZO & RAVIOLI BAKE

There's a little bit of care involved with this recipe as you need to pay attention to how you layer it up in the slow cooker, rather than just throwing it all in together. Once that's done though, it couldn't be easier and the result is cheesy, comforting goodness. You can play around with the veg and swap or add your favourites, but this is one of my go-tos. Gorgeous with a simple side salad.

SERVES **5**

150g chorizo, finely diced
400g tin of chopped
   tomatoes
2 courgettes, sliced
700g passata
1 tsp dried oregano
1 tsp dried thyme
1 red chilli, chopped
4 garlic cloves, chopped
   or grated

handful of fresh basil leaves
½ tsp paprika
500g shop-bought fresh
   ravioli (any filling you like)
80g light mozzarella, grated
1 tomato, thinly sliced
salt and pepper, to taste

1   Assemble the bake in the slow cooker. For the bottom layer, add your chorizo and tin of chopped tomatoes – heat rises, so the flavour of the chorizo will go through the upper layers. You can cook the chorizo first if you want to, but it's not necessary.

2   On top of that, add your sliced courgettes, almost to act as another layer, then top with the passata, dried herbs, chilli, garlic, fresh basil leaves and paprika.

3   Pop in your ravioli as the top layer and arrange in whatever shape or style you like, ensuring the ravioli are nicely tucked into the tomato sauce.

4   Cook on high for 2 hours or low for 4 hours.

5   Season well with salt and pepper, add the mozzarella, another sprinkle of pepper and layer over the thin slices of tomato. Pop the ovenproof slow-cooker pot (without the lid) under a hot grill for 7–8 minutes until golden and bubbling.

BAKED GNOCCHI & BLACK BEANS

PER SERVING
470
CALORIES

If you've read my previous books, you'll know I try to have one meat-free day per week. This is one of the dishes I go to again and again, and it's perfect if you're working from home. Simply load up the slow cooker at lunchtime, pop it on low for 4 hours, toss in your gnocchi and cheese and you're done. Gnocchi to me is pure comfort food, and this goes really well with a rocket and cucumber salad drizzled with balsamic vinegar and topped with seeds of your choice.

SERVES **4**

2 x 400g tins of black beans, drained
4 garlic cloves, grated
1 red onion, chopped
1 tbsp red pesto
700g passata
1 tsp paprika
handful of sundried tomatoes
1 tbsp dried oregano

handful of fresh basil, plus extra to garnish
500g fresh gnocchi
150ml vegetable stock, plus extra if needed
70g reduced-fat Cheddar cheese, grated
salt and pepper, to taste
salad and (optional) garlic bread, to serve

TIP
—
If you aren't bothered about going over 500 calories, garlic bread is perfect with this.

1   Add all the ingredients, except the gnocchi, stock and cheese, to the slow cooker. Cook on low for 4 hours or high for 2–2½ hours.

2   Add the gnocchi and stock and cook on high for another 30–40 minutes or on low for 60–80 minutes. If it looks a little dry at this point, add some more stock.

3   Top with the cheese, put the lid on and cook on high for another 10 minutes or low for 15 minutes.

4   Garnish with basil and serve with some salad.

CORONATION CHICKEN CURRY

When I think of coronation chicken, I think of it as a cold salad or delicious sandwich filling on a warm summer's day. However, served with rice and rotis for dipping and a gorgeous warm curry sauce, this takes comfort food a little bit further. Deliciously creamy and packed with flavour, say hello to your new favourite.

SERVES **4**

TIP
—
If you're in a rush, you can skip the first step of the method and just add the chicken and curry powder straight into the slow cooker in step 2. It'll taste just as delicious.

3 chicken breasts, cut into chunks
1 tbsp curry powder
low-calorie oil spray

Curry sauce
2 tbsp mango chutney
400ml tin of reduced-fat coconut milk
1 heaped tbsp ground turmeric
1 tsp curry powder
1 tsp ground cinnamon
3 garlic cloves, grated or chopped

2.5cm piece of fresh ginger, chopped or grated (I use frozen)
small handful of fresh coriander, finely chopped, plus extra to garnish
grated zest of ½ lime
1 tbsp sultanas

salt and pepper, to taste
chopped spring onions, to garnish
125g cooked basmati rice per person, to serve

1   Coat the chicken in the curry powder. Heat a frying pan over a medium heat on the hob and spray with low-calorie oil spray. Add the chicken and fry for 1 minute.

2   Add the chicken and all the curry sauce ingredients, except the sultanas, to the slow cooker. Cook on high for 3 hours or low for 5 hours. Add the sultanas for the last hour of cooking.

3   Garnish with fresh coriander and spring onions, and serve with rice.

CREAMY GARLIC CHICKEN

PER SERVING 371 CALORIES

This stunning recipe will have you coming back time and time again. Creamy garlic sauce with chicken is a match made in heaven. I serve this with rice or a wide pasta like tagliatelle which holds the sauce really well. If I have time, I'll seal the chicken breasts in a pan to give them some texture and elevate the flavour further, but if not, I'll just throw the chicken in raw and in chunks rather than the whole flattened breasts.

SERVES **4**

3–4 chicken breasts, flattened (around 400g)
1 tsp paprika
low-calorie oil spray
3 garlic cloves, grated
1 onion, chopped
230ml chicken stock
1 tbsp half-fat butter
½ tsp ground nutmeg
zest of ½ lemon

150g light soft cream cheese
1 tbsp cornflour mixed with 1 tbsp water (optional)
salt and pepper, to taste
chopped chives and cayenne pepper, to garnish (optional)
120g cooked tagliatelle per person, to serve

1   Coat the chicken in the paprika. Heat a frying pan over a medium heat on the hob and spray with low-calorie oil spray. Add the chicken and seal briefly for 2 minutes.

2   Add to the slow cooker with all the remaining ingredients, except the soft cheese, cornflour and pasta. Cook on high for 3–4 hours or low for 6 hours. Slice or pull apart the cooked chicken into pieces.

3   Stir in the soft cheese (if you'd like the sauce thicker, stir through the cornflour). Serve with pasta. Garnish with chives and, if you like heat, a dusting of cayenne pepper.

CHICKEN NORMANDY

PER SERVING
499
CALORIES

Chicken in a gorgeous creamy sauce with crispy cubed potatoes and greens. I mean, just imagine coming home to that after a long day. This will please anyone, any day of the week. If you aren't counting calories, I highly recommend swapping the chicken breasts for legs, and serving them with crunchy garlic bread to soak up any leftover sauce.

SERVES **4**

4 chicken breasts
1 tsp olive oil or low-calorie oil spray
fresh parsley, plus extra (optional) to garnish
1 tbsp half-fat butter
200ml cider
200ml chicken stock
1½ tbsp cornflour
3 garlic cloves, crushed
3 bay leaves
1 tbsp Dijon mustard

1 onion, chopped
200g bacon medallions, chopped, or lardons
5 sprigs of fresh thyme
3 tbsp light soft cream cheese or low-fat crème fraîche
salt and pepper, to taste
baked or air-fried cubed/ Parmentier potatoes and peas, to serve

1   Season your chicken with salt and pepper. Add the oil to a frying pan over a medium heat on the hob and briefly sear the chicken for 2 minutes until starting to go nice and brown.

2   Add to the slow cooker with all the remaining ingredients, except 2 sprigs of thyme and the soft cheese or crème fraîche. Cook on high for 4 hours or low for 7–8 hours.

3   Garnish with the reserved thyme or some parsley. This is perfect with baked or air-fried cubed potatoes and peas.

TIP

Frozen, pre-prepped garlic and onion can make this recipe even quicker to prep.

CHORIZO & SEAFOOD CHOWDER

PER SERVING
409
CALORIES

This gorgeous seafood bonanza with the flavour of salty chorizo is such a crowd-pleaser. Perfect with some warm Irish wheaten bread spread with butter. In Northern Ireland, we have access to the most incredible seafood, so if I see a version of this on a menu in a restaurant, the odds are I'll be ordering it.

SERVES **4**

100g chorizo, roughly chopped
300g cod fillet, skin removed and chopped into chunks
150g salmon fillet, skin removed and chopped into chunks
150g raw peeled prawns or shellfish of your choice
2 garlic cloves, grated
1 onion, chopped
zest and juice of 1 lemon
1 tbsp half-fat butter
½ tsp ground nutmeg
1 tsp Dijon mustard
handful of mixed fresh parsley and dill, chopped, plus extra parsley, to garnish

300ml skimmed milk
400ml chicken stock (or fish stock)
400g tin of garden peas
1 carrot, cut into chunks
300g potatoes, chopped into small-medium chunks
1 tbsp low-fat crème fraîche
1–2 tbsp cornflour, mixed to a paste with 1 tbsp water (optional – use 2 tbsp if you like it thick)
salt and pepper, to taste
1 slice of Irish wheaten bread per person, to serve (optional)

TIP
—

If you can't find Irish wheaten bread, just serve it with whatever bread you like.

1   Heat a frying pan over a medium heat and lightly fry the chorizo for 1–2 minutes.

2   Add all the ingredients, except the cornflour, to the slow cooker. Cook on high for 4 hours or low for 7 hours, adding the cornflour at the end, if required, to thicken further.

3   Garnish with some parsley and get stuck in.

RICH LAMB SHANKS

PER SERVING
429
CALORIES

When I think of a Sunday crowd-pleaser, then this is it, gorgeous tender chunks of lamb with a rich flavoursome gravy. I love serving this with minted peas and creamy mash, but crusty bread for dunking in the gravy is a great alternative. If you're looking to make this for a larger group, this recipe doubles really well to go around. If you're a family of four with two small kids, you could get away with just three lamb shanks.

SERVES **4**

1 tsp olive oil
4 lamb shanks
1 onion, chopped
1 carrot, chopped
100ml beef stock
2 x 400g tins of chopped
   tomatoes
2 tbsp tomato purée
1 red wine stock pot or
   splash of red wine

4 fresh mint leaves, chopped
2 bay leaves
handful each of fresh
   rosemary, thyme and
   oregano, leaves picked (or
   1 tbsp each dried)
1 tbsp cornflour, mixed to
   a paste with 1 tbsp water
salt and pepper, to taste

1   Massage the olive oil and some salt and pepper into the lamb shanks. Heat a frying pan over a medium heat on the hob and brown the lamb for 2 minutes.

2   Add the lamb to the slow cooker with all the remaining ingredients. Cook on high for 5 hours or low for 8 hours. Serve and enjoy.

SERVING NOTE

I love this with mash and minted peas.

SPICY STEAK VODKA RIGATONI

PER SERVING
476
CALORIES

This pasta dish has been trending for quite some time so I thought, why not make a slow-cooker version? Well, here it is. I've added some chilli and chipotle paste for an additional kick, so get your hanky ready as this packs a punch and will definitely blow the cobwebs away. I love a bit of spice during the colder months but, if you're not a fan, then just reduce the amount of chilli and chipotle or leave them out altogether.

SERVES **4**

low-calorie oil spray (optional)

400g lean steak, such as rump or any thin-cut steak, cut into strips

25ml vodka

1 red onion, sliced

1 tsp chilli powder (I use mild)

1 tbsp chipotle paste

1 tbsp dried oregano

1 tsp ground cumin

4 garlic cloves, grated

400g tin of chopped tomatoes

3 tbsp tomato purée

1 red pepper, sliced lengthways

1 green pepper, sliced lengthways

300g dried rigatoni

750ml chicken stock, plus extra if needed

3 tbsp light soft cream cheese

salt and pepper, to taste

1 sliced red chilli, to garnish

TIP

To make this quicker, you can skip the first step and add the steak in raw.

1   If you like a bit of char on your steak, heat a frying pan over a medium heat on the hob, spray with low-calorie oil spray and seal the steak for 2 minutes.

2   Add the steak, vodka, onion, chilli powder, chipotle paste, oregano, cumin, garlic, chopped tomatoes and tomato purée to the slow cooker and cook on high for 3 hours or low for 5–6 hours. If you cooked the steak on the hob, reduce the cooking time by 1 hour.

COMFORT FOOD

3 Stir in your sliced peppers, then add the rigatoni and chicken stock and cook on high for a further 40 minutes or low for an hour, without stirring. If it's looking dry, add another splash more stock.

4 Stir in the soft cheese and cook on high for a further 10 minutes or low for 15 minutes.

5 Garnish with the fresh chilli slices and enjoy.

CHOCOLATE & PEANUT BUTTER LAVA CAKE

PER SERVING
335
CALORIES

As a self-appointed slow-cooker expert, I have read a *lot* of books on cooking in the slow cooker and from time to time would come across a cake recipe. I decided to give it a go myself and, after a lot of retesting and refining, have landed on this recipe. The perfect slow-cooker cake, in my opinion. I use granulated sweetener to reduce the sugar content, dark chocolate and cocoa powder to make it extra rich and special, and peanut butter because who doesn't love peanut butter and chocolate together?

SERVES **8**

15g half-fat butter, softened, for greasing

Sponge
200g plain flour
100g light brown sugar
10g granulated sweetener
50g cocoa powder
2 tbsp powdered peanut butter or smooth from a jar
1 tsp baking powder
120g half-fat butter
70g chocolate chips (I prefer dark chocolate)
2 eggs

200ml skimmed milk
2 tsp vanilla extract
frozen yogurt, fresh mint leaves and chopped nuts, such as peanuts or hazelnuts, plus chocolate ice cream (optional), to serve

Topping
300ml boiling water
2 tbsp cocoa powder
2 tbsp white granulated sugar

1   Grease the slow cooker with the 15g of softened butter.

2   In a bowl, mix together the flour, sugar, sweetener, cocoa powder, peanut butter powder (if using jarred peanut butter, add in with your eggs and milk in the next step) and baking powder. Add this mixture to the slow cooker.

3   Melt the butter and chocolate chips in a heatproof bowl in the microwave for 1–2 minutes. While this is melting, beat

TIP

If you can't find powdered peanut butter (it's usually sold alongside things like protein bars), smooth peanut butter is fine to use instead but it will increase the calories.

the eggs, milk and vanilla extract together, then add the melted butter mixture and jarred peanut butter, if using. Once combined, add the wet mixture to the slow cooker and stir well until a batter is formed.

4   For the topping, mix the boiling water, cocoa powder and sugar in a jug and pour over the batter. Please do not stir once you have added the saucy goodness, just let it do its thing.

5   Put the lid on and cook on high for 2¼ hours or low for 4½ hours – do not remove the lid at any stage, no matter how tempting it may be.

6   Serve with some frozen yogurt, mint leaves and chopped nuts. Feel free to add some chocolate ice cream to make it extra boujee. The cake will absorb the sauce on serving, so don't wait around and get stuck in.

FEEDING A CROWD

PORK CARNITA NACHOS

PER SERVING
490
CALORIES

This versatile pulled pork can be used for nachos, as I've done here, or for tacos, burritos, or whatever you fancy – it works so well with them all. This is a simplified version of carnitas, the Mexican pulled pork dish. I've suggested pork shoulder steaks, which are a leaner cut, but if calories aren't a concern, then regular pork shoulder will be even tastier. This is enough for two large platters, so be prepared to win the best-host-ever award.

SERVES **10**

2kg pork shoulder steaks (or you can use pork shoulder)
1 tbsp ground cumin
1 tsp dried oregano
1 bay leaf
200ml light beer (I use Corona)
400ml chicken stock
1 tsp chipotle paste
4 garlic cloves, crushed or sliced
zest and juice of 2 limes
1 lemon, cut into quarters
1 slice of orange

400g salted tortilla chips
50g reduced-fat Cheddar cheese, grated
salt and pepper, to taste
300g jar of sweety drop peppers (drained), sliced red onion, fresh coriander and (optional) soured cream, to garnish
1 medium avocado and handful of cherry tomatoes, cut into chunks, to serve

1   Dry the pork with some kitchen paper. Coat the pork in the cumin and oregano and add to the slow cooker with the bay leaf, beer, stock, chipotle paste, garlic, lime zest and juice, lemon and orange. Cook on high for 7–8 hours or low for 10 hours.

2   Shred the pork with two forks, discarding the bay leaf and fruit.

3   Heat your nachos if you like – you could pop the tortilla chips in the air fryer at 180°C for 2 minutes or just add to 2 large baking trays. Layer up the tortilla chips, then the

cheese, then the pork. You could also pop the trays in the oven at 180°C for 10 minutes.

4   Top the nachos with the sweety drop peppers, red onion, fresh coriander and even some soured cream, if you like. I serve some mixed chopped avo and cherry tomatoes on the side for anyone who likes a sprinkle.

TIP

▬▬

Only the cooked pork will freeze, not the tortilla chips or toppings.

SWEET COCKTAIL SAUSAGE STEW

PER SERVING
463
CALORIES

The beauty of writing a cookbook is you get to experiment and eat all this gorgeous food before anyone else does. This is probably my favourite recipe in the book, I am obsessed. This gets its inspiration from a tagine, which is more traditionally made with lamb. The fruit in the sauce gives a lovely sweetness that goes so well with the depth of the spices. Served with couscous and topped with fresh mint, perfection.

SERVES **6**

1 tsp olive oil or low-calorie oil spray
450g raw cocktail sausages (or turkey or regular sausages)
1 ripe mango, peeled and finely chopped
1 red chilli, sliced
1 tbsp mango chutney
75g pitted green olives
1 tsp ground ginger
1 tsp ground cinnamon
1 tbsp garlic granules
zest and juice of 1 lemon

600g passata
1 tsp ground coriander
1 tsp onion granules (or 1 onion, chopped)
1 tbsp tomato purée
pinch of saffron strands
100ml chicken stock
salt and pepper, to taste
handful of fresh mint leaves, to garnish
600g cooked couscous mixed with chopped tomatoes, radishes, spring onions and fresh mint, to serve

TIP
—

Make a vegetarian version of this by swapping for veggie sausages and veg stock.

1   Add the olive oil or low-calorie oil spray to a frying pan over a medium heat on the hob and seal the sausages for 1–2 minutes.

2   Transfer to the slow cooker with all the remaining ingredients (except the mint and couscous salad). Cook on high for 4 hours or low for 7–8 hours.

3   Garnish with the fresh mint and serve with the couscous.

SWEET & SPICY CHICKEN CURRY
with lime rice

This is based on the classic Cape Malay curry, which originated in South Africa from the enslaved Indonesian and Indian population. It's a flavour overload, perfect for wowing guests with. Just trust me when I say, invite some friends over and watch this curry completely blow their minds. It's a must-try.

SERVES **5**

600g boneless chicken thighs, cut into chunks
1 onion, chopped
1 tbsp half-fat butter
1 tsp dried chilli flakes
1 tbsp ground cardamom or ground nutmeg
1 tbsp curry powder
1 tsp ground turmeric
1 cinnamon stick
1 tsp garam masala
1 heaped tbsp garlic purée
2 x 400g tins of chopped tomatoes
1 tbsp honey

100ml chicken stock
juice of 1 lime
400g baby potatoes, cut into chunks
salt and pepper, to taste
fresh coriander leaves, to garnish

Lime rice
250g dried basmati rice
1 cinnamon stick
1 bay leaf
zest and juice of 2 limes
1 heaped tbsp ground turmeric

1   Add all the ingredients (except the coriander and rice ingredients) to the slow cooker. Cook on high for 4 hours or low for 7–8 hours. The flavour will intensify the longer it cooks.

2   For the lime rice, cook the rice according to the packet instructions, adding all the rice ingredients to the pan too. Discard the cinnamon stick and bay leaf before serving.

3   Remove the cinnamon stick from the curry, garnish with fresh coriander and serve with the lime rice.

TURKEY MEATBALL & TOMATO BAKE

Who doesn't love meatballs and tomato sauce? It's such a classic combination, and this is a leaner version using turkey mince rather than the classic beef. If you can't find turkey mince, chicken would work equally well. Paired with your favourite salad, pasta or some crunchy garlic bread, this is the ultimate crowd-pleaser.

SERVES **5**

Meatballs

600g turkey or chicken mince

80g panko breadcrumbs

1 egg

large handful of fresh basil, chopped, plus extra to garnish

3 heaped tbsp ricotta cheese

2 garlic cloves, grated

Tomato sauce

2 red peppers, chopped

100ml chicken stock

700g passata

3 tbsp tomato purée

1 garlic clove, grated

1 red onion, chopped

zest of 1 lemon

1 courgette, chopped

handful of sundried tomatoes, chopped

5 cherry tomatoes, chopped

1 tsp paprika

70g reduced-fat mozzarella, sliced

salt and pepper, to taste

grated Parmesan cheese, to serve

1   In a large bowl, mix together all the meatball ingredients. Roll the mixture into meatballs as small or large as you like.

2   Briefly cook the meatballs in a frying pan over a medium heat on the hob for 1–2 minutes until they start to go a bit brown on the sides.

3   Add all the remaining ingredients, except the mozzarella, to the slow cooker, then pop the meatballs on top, adding some extra basil leaves for some punch. Cook on high for 3–4 hours or low for 5 hours.

4   Top with the mozzarella slices and pop the lid back on for
10 minutes. Garnish with more fresh basil, finish with grated
Parmesan and serve.

TIP
▬▬

You can pair this with linguine pasta or just
a salad; I do love a watermelon and feta salad
with this recipe.

STICKY HOISIN PORK BAO BUNS

EACH
225
CALORIES

Pulled pork is always a really popular slow-cooker recipe and this version is enriched with soy, honey and hoisin. It's so flavourful, I cannot get enough, especially when piled into soft, pillowy bao buns. This is sweet and spicy deliciousness, finished with some added fresh sweetness from the pomegranate seeds.

MAKES **8–10**

600g pork fillet, left whole (or another cut)
low-calorie oil spray
2 tbsp dark soy sauce
3 tbsp honey
3 tbsp hoisin sauce
1 tsp rice vinegar
1 tsp sesame oil
4 garlic cloves, grated
1 tsp chilli flakes
1 tbsp orange juice or Chinese rice wine
300ml chicken stock

handful of chopped Thai basil, plus extra to garnish (or any fresh basil or 1 tbsp dried basil)
1 tbsp cornflour mixed with 1 tbsp water (optional)
salt and pepper, to taste
fresh coriander and pomegranate seeds, to garnish
8–10 shop-bought bao buns, heated in the microwave or steamed, to serve

1   Season the pork with salt and pepper. Heat a frying pan over a medium heat on the hob, spray with low-calorie oil spray, then add the pork and seal for 1–2 minutes.

2   Add to the slow cooker with all the remaining ingredients, except the cornflour and bao buns. Cook on high for 5–6 hours or low for 8 hours. Baste the pork a few times throughout if you can. If you want the sauce thicker, add the cornflour at the end.

3   Shred the pork with two forks, then chuck back into the pot to coat in the sauce. Serve in the bao buns with fresh coriander and some pomegranate seeds to balance the heat.

CHORIZO CARBONARA ORZO

PER SERVING
437
CALORIES

I love a carbonara as much as the next person and while making it with bacon medallions will reduce your calories, chorizo just elevates it to a new place. This version is a twist with the addition of peas and orzo instead of the more traditional spaghetti. Perfect to serve as a starter if you've got people round.

SERVES **6**

200g chorizo, chopped into chunks
1 shallot or small onion, finely chopped
juice of 1 lemon
1 garlic clove, grated
1.3 litres chicken or veg stock, plus extra if needed
100g frozen peas or 1 leek, chopped

300g dried orzo
100g light soft cream cheese
75g Parmesan cheese, grated
salt and pepper, to taste
chopped fresh parsley, to garnish
cheesy garlic bread, to serve (optional)

1   Add the chorizo, shallot, lemon juice, garlic, some salt and pepper and 100ml of the chicken stock to the slow cooker. We don't want to drown the dish by adding all the stock at once, just enough moisture to let it cook nicely. Cook on high for 2 hours or low for 4 hours. (If you are using a leek instead of peas, add this from the start.)

2   Then add the remaining stock, the peas, if using, and the orzo and cook on high for a further 50 minutes. Check after 40 minutes if you need to add another 100ml of water.

3   Stir in the soft cheese and 50g of the Parmesan cheese until mixed through.

4   Add to your bowls, top with fresh parsley and the remaining Parmesan and serve with cheesy garlic bread, if you like.

VEGGIE JALFREZI

PER SERVING
447
CALORIES

This is the speediest jalfrezi imaginable; the ultimate 'throw-and-go' dish. This is one of my go-to veggie curries but that doesn't mean you can't use chicken or lamb. Whatever you choose, just be warned this spice mix is amazing but packs some serious heat. This curry itself comes in at around 100 calories per serving, leaving lots of room for rice and naan.

SERVES **6**

700g frozen chopped mixed vegetables, such as carrot, cauliflower and sweet potato (around 200g of each veg)
1 onion, chopped
1 tbsp ground cumin
1 tbsp ground coriander
1 tbsp garam masala
1 tbsp ground turmeric
1 tsp ground ginger
4 garlic cloves, crushed or sliced

1 green chilli, sliced
1 red chilli, sliced, plus extra (chopped) to garnish
100ml vegetable stock
2 x 400g tins of chopped tomatoes
handful of fresh coriander, chopped, plus extra to garnish
salt and pepper, to taste
125g cooked basmati rice and ½ large naan per person, to serve

1   Add all the ingredients, except the coriander and the rice, to the slow cooker. Cook on high for 4 hours or low for 7–8 hours.

2   Garnish with extra chopped red chilli and fresh coriander. Serve with rice and naan.

TIP

To make a chicken or lamb jalfrezi, swap the frozen mixed veg for 500g of diced raw meat and cook as above.

COQ AU VIN CHICKEN POT ROAST

PER SERVING
240
CALORIES

While this moreish recipe feels like a colder-month staple, it is perfect all year round. Served with greens and mash, it really is a perfect dish for hosting; it will always go down well. I use mash if I'm making this in the winter, but during the summer it goes equally well with some couscous and peas.

SERVES **6**

2 smoked bacon medallions, chopped
1 tsp half-fat butter
1 medium chicken (around 1.2kg)
1 red wine stock pot or splash of red wine
400ml beef stock
2 shallots, sliced
250g whole button mushrooms

5 garlic cloves, peeled and left whole
2 carrots, chopped
2 sprigs of thyme
2 sprigs of rosemary
1 tbsp tomato purée
2 tbsp gravy granules
cooked peas and greens of your choice, plus (optional) mashed potatoes, to serve

1   Use a pair of scissors to quickly chop up your bacon medallions. In a frying pan over a medium heat on the hob, melt the butter and cook the bacon for 2 minutes.

2   Add the bacon to the slow cooker with all the remaining ingredients, except the gravy granules. Cook on high for 5 hours or low for 8 hours.

3   Stir in the gravy granules and pop the ovenproof slow-cooker pot (without the lid) under a hot grill for 10 minutes to crisp up the chicken skin.

4   Serve with peas and greens, and mashed potatoes, if you like.

GOCHUJANG PORK TACOS

PER SERVING
432
CALORIES

One thing I'll never get bored of is tacos: any flavour, form, shape, soft shell or hard, I am not remotely fussy. I could honestly eat them every day, and these gorgeous rich and sticky tacos will have you coming back time and time again. This makes a good amount of pork, so will feed all the family, and it's perfect for having guests over too.

SERVES 10

1kg pork shoulder (in one piece), skin removed but reserved if you like
4 tbsp gochujang paste
200ml chicken stock
2 tbsp sriracha
4 tbsp reduced-sugar tomato ketchup
1 tbsp dark soy sauce
1 tbsp hoisin sauce

1 tsp brown sugar
1 onion, chopped
3 garlic cloves, grated
1 tsp sesame oil
salt and pepper, to taste
2 corn tacos per person, sweetcorn salsa, cucumber slices and chopped red onion, to serve

TIP

Use some of the leftover sauce from the slow-cooker pot if you want your meat to be a bit juicier. These are also great with a bit of gochujang mayo.

1   Add all the ingredients except the tacos and serving accompaniments to the slow cooker. Cook on high for 5–6 hours or low for 8–9 hours.

2   For an extra garnish, crisp up the pork skin in an air fryer at 200°C for 30 minutes or in the oven for 50 minutes.

3   Shred the pork using two forks. Pair the pork with your tacos and sweetcorn salsa, cucumber slices and red onion. Bring the tacos back to life by holding them (using tongs) over a gas hob for 15 seconds on each side.

SMOKY BEEF GOULASH WITH CHORIZO

PER SERVING 499 CALORIES

I love a beef goulash and apologise to all of Hungary right now for giving it this Spanish twist. You'll know by now how obsessed I am with chorizo and I love the smoky spice it brings to this dish. Goulash is versatile, you can serve it with pasta, mash, rice or just have it on its own with a salad or some steamed green veg.

SERVES **6**

1kg stewing or braising steak, cut into chunks
100g chorizo, chopped
600ml beef stock
1 tbsp paprika
1 onion, chopped
handful of fresh parsley, chopped, plus extra to garnish
50ml red wine or 1 red wine stock pot
3 tbsp tomato purée
400g tin of chopped tomatoes

4 large tomatoes, quartered
3 garlic cloves, crushed or sliced
1 tbsp cornflour
1 red pepper, chopped
1 green pepper, chopped
soured cream, to garnish
150g creamy mashed potato per person, to serve

1   If you have time and want to elevate the flavour, heat a frying pan over a medium heat on the hob and seal the beef for 1 minute.

2   Add to the slow cooker with all the remaining ingredients, except the peppers. Cook on high for 4 hours or low for 7 hours.

3   For the last 30 minutes, add the peppers.

4   Garnish with soured cream and fresh parsley and serve with the mash.

PORK WITH A CREAMY APPLE SAUCE

Pork and apple is such a dream combo, and a great way to impress if you've got friends round. It also makes a nice alternative on Christmas day if you're not a turkey fan. I suggest searing the pork before adding it to the slow cooker so you get that gorgeous char on the outside, which goes beautifully with the creamy apple sauce. Serve this with boiled baby potatoes or roasties with some green beans.

SERVES **5**

1 tsp half-fat butter

700g pork fillet or tenderloin, left whole (or pork chops, sausages or whatever you have)

2 green apples, cored and diced (I use Granny Smith)

3 garlic cloves, grated

100ml chicken stock

100ml apple juice or cider

1 tsp Dijon mustard

½ tsp ground nutmeg

1 tsp dried sage

1 tsp dried thyme

1 shallot, finely chopped

3 tbsp half-fat crème fraîche

1 tbsp cornflour mixed with 1 tbsp water (optional)

salt and pepper, to taste

100g green beans and 175g boiled baby potatoes per person, to serve

1   Melt the butter in a frying pan over a medium heat on the hob. Add the pork and sear for 2 minutes until you start to see that gorgeous brown char.

2   Add the pork and all the remaining ingredients, except the crème fraîche and cornflour, to the slow cooker. Cook on high for 4 hours or low for 6–7 hours.

3   For the last 5 minutes, stir in the crème fraîche to get the sauce creamy. If you need to thicken the sauce, stir in the cornflour. Slice the pork before serving.

4   Serve with green beans and baby potatoes.

STEAK & GUINNESS PIE

PER SERVING
439
CALORIES

Being Irish, it won't be a surprise that I love Guinness or that I love pies. Traditionally-made pies can be a bit of a labour of love, but this is the easiest pie recipe you'll ever make – just throw it in, let it cook away during the day, add a pastry lid and serve. It is honestly that easy. It's gorgeously rich, and a beef gravy pie is something truly special, perfect on a cold day.

SERVES **6**

800g beef steak or rump (or 1kg brisket), chopped
440ml can of Guinness
200ml beef stock
1 tbsp tomato purée
1 tsp dried rosemary
1 tsp dried thyme
1 tsp dried oregano
1 bay leaf
1 tbsp brown sugar
2 carrots, roughly chopped
1 red onion, chopped

1 celery stick, chopped
1 heaped tbsp cornflour
3 garlic cloves, crushed
1 sheet of ready-rolled puff pastry
1 egg, beaten, to glaze the pastry
salt and pepper, to taste
Tenderstem broccoli and carrot and parsnip mash, to serve (optional)

TIP

To get the pastry the right size, put your slow-cooker lid on top of your puff pastry sheet and cut round it before adding to the slow cooker.

1   Throw all the ingredients, except the pastry and egg, in the slow cooker.

2   Cook on high for 4 hours or low for 7–8 hours. Discard the bay leaf.

3   Preheat the oven to 200°C. Top the beef filling with the puff pastry, tuck it round the pie, then brush with the beaten egg. Pop the ovenproof slow-cooker pot (without the lid) into the oven for 25 minutes until golden and crisp. If your slow-cooker pot isn't oven-safe, decant the filling into an ovenproof pot, cover with the pastry, brush with the egg and bake as above.

4   Serve with Tenderstem broccoli and carrot and parsnip mash, if you like.

STICKY BALSAMIC & CHERRY COLA HAM BRIOCHE BUNS

If anyone tells you a cola ham is just for Christmas, unfriend them, immediately. I guarantee this will have people coming back for more, whatever the season. Sticky ham cooked in cherry cola, basted with a sweet balsamic and mustard glaze, I'm getting hungry just writing this. Stuffed into a toasted brioche bun, this is perfect for a pack-up-and-go lunch for a crowd.

SERVES **10**

1.5kg boneless gammon joint
700ml cherry cola (ideally diet)
handful of cherries, pierced with a fork (optional)
1 cinnamon stick
1 bay leaf
10 brioche buns, cut in half and toasted
shredded lettuce or greens
red coleslaw (you can make your own but shop-bought is perfect for speed)

Glaze
1 tbsp Dijon mustard
3 tbsp honey
1 tbsp brown sugar
1 tbsp balsamic vinegar

1   If you like, you can soak the gammon in cold water overnight to remove the excess salt.

2   When ready to cook, add the gammon, cola, cherries, cinnamon stick and bay leaf to the slow cooker. Cook on high for 4–5 hours or low for 7–8 hours. Allow to cool.

3   Preheat the oven to 190°C. Combine the glaze ingredients. Trim the gammon fat and score in a diamond pattern. Place the gammon on a baking tray and brush with the glaze. Cook for 25 minutes, basting regularly in the glaze. You can also air-fry at 160°C for 15–20 minutes – watch it doesn't burn.

4   To serve, slice the gammon, then add to the toasted buns with some lettuce or greens and coleslaw.

NO-KNEAD OLIVE & ROSEMARY BREAD

PER SERVING
244
CALORIES

It's my rule that every soup needs to be served with bread on the side and I wanted to create a perfect slow-cooker loaf to go with the soups in this book. Now, if I'm out for dinner and there's an olive and rosemary bread on the menu, you can bet I'll be ordering it. This version is so good and you don't even need to knead it – just make it the night before and throw into your slow cooker. Making bread doesn't get any easier.

SERVES **10**

700g strong white flour, plus extra for dusting

7–8g (1 sachet) fast-action dried yeast

2 tsp sea salt

1 tsp white granulated sugar

500ml lukewarm water (not too warm)

2 handfuls of chopped or whole olives, pitted

2 sprigs of fresh rosemary, leaves picked and chopped

1 tsp olive oil (optional)

TIP

You will get a better rise on the bread if you knead it before putting it in the slow cooker, but trust me, it tastes just as good made both ways.

1   In a large bowl, mix together the flour, yeast, salt and sugar, creating a small well in the middle with your spoon. Stir in the water and mix well with a wooden spoon.

2   Add the olives and most of the rosemary. Cover the bowl with clingfilm and leave for at least 10–12 hours or overnight, if possible, at room temperature or in the fridge.

3   Preheat your slow cooker on high so it's warm as soon as the dough hits it; I find this helps give a better result.

4   If you're not able to rest the dough, knead it on a floured surface for 8–10 minutes. Shape the dough into a ball and line your slow-cooker pot with a piece of baking paper or tin foil, ensuring the sides are covered too. This helps prevent the bread from sticking to the slow-cooker pot.

5   Sprinkle with the reserved rosemary and score on the top, if you wish.

6   Add the dough to the slow-cooker pot and cook on high for 2 hours 20 minutes or low for 3 hours 20 minutes – do not remove the lid at any stage during cooking.

7   For a crispy golden crust, remove the lid, brush the top of the loaf with the olive oil and air-fry at 160°C for 5 minutes or just pop it on a baking tray in a 160°C oven for 20 minutes.

8   Cool the loaf slightly, then slice to serve.

PANTRY ESSENTIALS

Here I've included a list of some of my most-used ingredients that I try to have on hand so that I can create tasty, healthy food at home. It's not an exhaustive list and you definitely don't need to go out and buy them all at once. These are just some of the staples I aim to have in stock and recommend that you do too.

FOR FLAVOUR
- Dried herbs – oregano, basil, thyme, rosemary, coriander
- Paprika, chilli flakes, garlic granules, onion granules, chilli powder
- Salt and pepper

FOR FAKEAWAY RECIPES
- Soy sauce, hoisin sauce, honey, rice vinegar, tins of reduced-fat coconut milk, sriracha, peanut butter
- Garlic and ginger – use fresh, dried, frozen or purée from a jar

SAUCE ESSENTIALS
- Stocks including vegetable, chicken and beef
- Cornflour to help you thicken a sauce
- Tins of chopped tomatoes or bottles/ jars of passata
- Tomato purée
- Worcestershire sauce

TO FILL YOU UP
- Rice
- Lentils
- Dried pasta – for the slow cooker, penne, farfalle and orzo all work really well. (You can also use fresh pasta but this will take about a third of the time to cook as dried pasta.) Adding the pasta directly into your slow cooker, rather than cooking it separately on the hob, reduces the need for boiling a kettle and saves on extra washing up
- Sweet potatoes
- Baby potatoes and standard potatoes
- Tinned beans (various)
- Noodles (egg or rice)

FRESH INGREDIENTS FOR EVEN MORE FLAVOUR
- Coriander leaves
- Basil leaves
- Rosemary sprigs
- Parsley
- Thyme sprigs
- Lemons, limes and oranges
- Onions

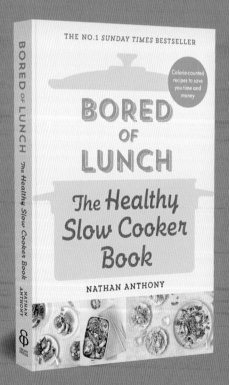

ACKNOWLEDGEMENTS

There's a huge team of people that make BOL tick and help to make it what it is. Thank you to Kyle for being the most patient person I know, and to Celia Palazzo, Alice King, Dem Scanlon and Steph Reynolds for helping me to achieve things I never thought would be possible, especially for a home cook from Northern Ireland.

To the incredible shoot team, Dan, Natalie, Max, Jodene, Lucy and Caitlin. When I think of this book, I'll think of your favourite Taylor Swift songs playing constantly in the studio; you may even have converted me to a fully-fledged Swiftie.

Finally and most importantly, to my readers and online followers who have made this all happen. I feel very blessed and lucky that I get to go on this exciting journey and continue connecting people around the world through the medium of food and recipes, so thank you to all of you for buying a copy of this book.

Nathan x

5 7 9 10 8 6 4

Ebury Press,
an imprint of Ebury Publishing
20 Vauxhall Bridge Road
London SW1V 2SA

Ebury Press is part of the Penguin Random House group
of companies whose addresses can be found at global.
penguinrandomhouse.com

First published by Ebury Press in 2024

www.penguin.co.uk

A CIP catalogue record for this book is available from the British
Library

ISBN 9781529914474

Commissioning Editor: Celia Palazzo
Production Director: Catherine Ngwong
Design: maru studio G.K.
Photographer: Dan Jones
Food stylists: Natalie Thomson and Jodene Jordan
Prop stylist: Max Robinson

Printed and bound in Italy by Printer Trento s.r.l.
The authorised representative in the EEA is Penguin Random House
Ireland, Morrison Chambers, 32 Nassau Street, Dublin D02 YH68.

'Healthy recipes that are delicious and easy to do.'

Laura McAllister

'I no longer need takeaways in my life.'

Sarah McClurg

'Accelerated my weight loss journey as a single mum.'

Sophie Kate

'Life-changing!'

Sinead Wheatley

'Budget friendly and timesaving.'

Nuala O'Connell